Compassion in Tibetan Buddhism

Compassion in Tibetan Buddhism

Tsong-ka-pa

With Kensur Lekden's
Meditations of a Tantric Abbot

EDITED AND TRANSLATED BY
Jeffrey Hopkins

Co-editor for Tsong-ka-pa's text: Lati Rinbochay
Associate editor for Kensur Lekden's text: Barbara Frye
Assistant editors for Tsong-ka-pa's text: Anne Klein
and Elizabeth Napper

Snow Lion Publications
Ithaca, New York, U.S.A.

Snow Lion Publications
P.O. Box 6483
Ithaca, New York 14851 U.S.A.

First Published 1980
by Rider and Company, London

First Published in U.S.A. 1980
Second Printing 1982
Gabriel/Snow Lion
Third Printing 1985
Snow Lion Publications
Printed in U.S.A.

Introduction © Jeffrey Hopkins 1980
Translation © Jeffrey Hopkins 1980

Library of Congress Catalog
Card Number 80-85453

ISBN-0-937938-04-1

Contents

Acknowledgement

The translator wishes to thank Mr Gerald Yorke for many suggestions that improved the rendering in English.

Technical Note

The transliteration scheme for Sanskrit names and titles is aimed at easy pronunciation, using *sh*, *ṣh*, and *ch* rather than *ś*, *ṣ*, and *c*. With the first occurrence of each Indian title, the Sanskrit is given, if available. Often Tsong-ka-pa refers only to the title or the author of a work, whereas both are given in translation to obviate checking back and forth. The full Sanskrit and Tibetan titles are to be found in the bibliography which is arranged alphabetically according to the English titles of sutras and according to the authors of other works. The Sanskrit and Tibetan for key terminology have been included in a glossary at the end.

Preface

Homage to Manjushri and Sarasvati.

Kensur Lekden (1900–71) was abbot of the Tantric College of Lower Lhasa prior to the invasion of Tibet by the Chinese Communists. At the time of the invasion, he had already been elevated to the position of 'abbot emeritus' and, after fleeing to India, helped to re-establish centres of Buddhist learning and meditation in India. Events brought him to France where he tutored several Tibetan monks, and in 1968 he came to a Tibetan and Mongolian Buddhist monastery in Freewood Acres, New Jersey, founded by Geshe Wangyal. In February of 1970 he was invited to teach at Tibet House in Cambridge, Wisconsin, founded by the late Professor Richard Robinson and myself, where I served as his translator.

Kensur Lekden, an embodiment of the unified practice of sutra and tantra and transmitter of the ancient Tibetan knowledge of meditation, taught at Tibet House for a year and a half. In a series of lectures in the spring of 1970, he set forth the paths common to sutra and tantra, freely and intimately, as part of the transmission of Buddhism to the West. Part One of this book is comprised of those lectures. Part Two is a translation of the first five chapters of Tsong-ka-pa's commentary to Chandrakirti's *Supplement to the Middle Way (Madhyamakāvatāra)*, which Kensur Lekden taught me, along with Jam-yang-shay-ba's sub-commentary, while at Tibet House. The short introduction to Part Two is from his and the Dalai Lama's oral teachings. The chapter divisions and other titles in Tsong-ka-pa's text were added to facilitate understanding, and for the same reason Chandrakirti's verses have been inserted into the commentary.

The combination of Kensur Lekden's meditations and Tsong-ka-pa's detailed explanation affords a unique blend of the oral and written traditions of Tibetan Buddhism on the principal motivation for enlightenment, compassion. Vast from the viewpoint of setting forth the compassionate deeds of Bodhisat-tvas (heroes with respect to contemplating enlightenment) and profound from the viewpoint of presenting the empty nature of phenomena, these teachings shine with the sun of Buddha's doctrine reflected so brightly in snowy Tibet.

JEFFREY HOPKINS
Charlottesville, Virginia

PART ONE

Meditations of a Tantric Abbot

KENSUR LEKDEN

Introduction

In Buddhism persons are identified from the viewpoint of capacity – great, middling, or small. The small of the small do not practise any religion, but only strive for happiness in this present existence. Like animals, these beings do not achieve any virtue at all.

The middling of the small engage in both religious and non-religious means to achieve happiness in the present for only themselves, not for their friends or even for their own future lives. Due to this low motivation, their activities cannot function as religious practice.

The great of the small engage in virtue, seeking happiness, comfort, food, drink, resources, and so forth mainly for future lives. Because they practise not for the sake of others but for their own temporary welfare in cyclic existence – the beginningless round of birth, ageing, sickness, and death – they are the lowest among actual religious practitioners, but due to their longer perspective are included within the count of actual devotees.

They have identified the cause and effect of actions as well as their own virtues and non-virtues. They know that in their next life they will experience pleasures as gods or humans from virtuous deeds done in this lifetime and will experience sufferings as hell-beings, hungry ghosts, or animals from non-virtuous deeds done in this lifetime. They realize that at best this existence will not last more than a hundred years and that there are innumerable births in the future. Therefore, rather than seek their own welfare in this lifetime, which is so short, they begin to engage in religious practice for the sake of future lives.

Initially, they go for refuge from the depths of their hearts to the Three Jewels, relying on Buddha, his Doctrine, and the Spiritual Community for protection and help. This is done with strong intention because they have concern for their own suffering in bad migrations and believe that the Three Jewels have the power to protect them. Their concern and belief make the act of refuge not just verbal but actual.

The verbal formula is:

I go for refuge to the Lama.
I go for refuge to the Buddha.
I go for refuge to the Doctrine.
I go for refuge to the Spiritual Community.

Although there are Three Jewels, not four, we put 'I go for refuge to the Lama' first for a reason. When in his eighty-first year Buddha informed his students that he was about to die, Manjushri and Vajrapani asked him, 'When you die, from whom can we request doctrine? On whom can we rely? It is very difficult to judge a person from his external shape; we will not know what to do.'

Buddha said, 'When in the future you request the teaching of doctrine from another, I will bless and enter the form of your guru [*lama* in Tibetan]. If you have faith that he is I, that will serve as faith in me.' Since that time, refuge has also been taken in the guru, with the sense not that he is separate from the Three Jewels but that he is the embodiment of them.

Whether a person has refuge or not is determined by four qualities:

1 whether he knows the attributes of the Three Jewels
2 knows their differences
3 accepts them as the pure source of refuge
4 will not propound any other source of refuge.

Buddha is the teacher of refuge. The actual refuge is the Doctrine, comprised of training in the paths of ethics, meditative stabilization, and wisdom, and the nirvanas attained through these paths. The Spiritual Community are the monks, nuns, and laypersons who are one's helpers on the way to refuge. When understanding of these has formed, one has continuous refuge whether working, studying, eating, or even sleeping.

The best among those of small capacity have much to think about at this point. They wonder if attainment of a good future life is sufficient; they see that even if, through seeking the help of the Three Jewels, they attain the life of a god or human in their next lifetime, they will be born, grow old, become sick, and die. They arrive at the great understanding that merely gaining happiness in the next lifetime is not sufficient.

A person exceeds the thought of a being of small capacity when he realizes that there is no peace until he no longer has to be reborn through the force of contaminated actions and afflictions. Progressing, he decides to obtain liberation from all types of cyclic existence and seeks the bliss of the extinguishment of suffering. Further, since the causes of contaminated actions are the afflictions of desire, hatred, and ignorance, he identifies these as foes and, by aiming to overcome them, generates the attitude of a being with middling capacity. Through proper meditation he can then be liberated from cyclic existence as a Foe Destroyer (*Arhan*).

He attains a peace which is an extinguishment of all suffering; freed from cyclic existence, he does not need resources, food, or clothing, nor does he need sleep. Never again reborn and beyond ageing, sickness, and death, he can stay in trance for even a thousand aeons, and it seems like only an hour. However, he does not help other sentient beings and is far from achieving Buddhahood. Thus, the Buddhas rouse a Foe Destroyer from meditative stabilization and cause him to enter the Mahayana as a being of great capacity.

There are cases in the mountain-cave retreats of India and Tibet where those who have spent an aeon in meditative stabilization have finally left their bodies. While they were meditating, their fingernails wrapped around their bodies many times. A corpse, with fingernails encircling it, is all that is left for others to see after the Buddhas have caused them to rise. Such practice is a protracted path because those who pass from the level of the best of the small directly to the level of great capacity attain Buddhahood much faster.

These latter realize that attaining the happiness of a god or a human in the next lifetime is not sufficient either for themselves or for others. They are concerned about four faults in all sentient beings:

1 cyclic existence
2 the seeking of a solitary peace that is mere liberation for their own sake
3 obstructions to liberation
4 obstructions to omniscience.

They believe that the Three Jewels have the power to protect all beings from these four faults and go for refuge to Buddha, his Doctrine, and the Spiritual Community from the depths of the heart.

Intent upon the welfare of others, they have forsaken their own welfare, which then is accomplished as it could not be in any other way. For example, when the head of a country forsakes his own welfare and is intent upon that of others, his own country benefits greatly; in seeking peace for the world, he himself becomes famous and respected. Similarly, in altruistic endeavour, happiness spontaneously arises along the way even though no effort is made on one's own behalf.

Because of the difference in motivation, one instance of refuge by the great is more powerful than a hundred thousand refuges by the small. Thus, whether hearing, thinking, or meditating, one should precede all practice with the refuge of a being of great capacity.

I am concerned about all sentient beings. I am concerned about their cyclic existence, solitary peace, and two obstructions, and I believe that the Three Jewels have the power to protect all sentient beings from these faults. From the depths of my heart I ask the Three Jewels for help.

1 *Action*

Because humans are doers of deeds, Buddhism explains how to act – how to adopt the means to make oneself and others happy. This involves hearing, thinking, and meditating. Hearing means to listen to the explanations of a guru or read books in order to discover what is to be practised and why.

One finds that over the continuum of lives one needs the body of a human or a god – healthy and free from suffering – the resources necessary to maintain that body, long life, and the power to achieve what one wants. The main cause of such high status within the round of birth, aging, sickness, and death is proper ethics; as Chandrakirti says in his *Supplement to the Middle Way* (stanza 24)

> . . . a cause of definite goodness
> And high status is none other than proper ethics.

Proper ethics give rise to the great fortune of possessing a human or divine body rather than the body of an animal, hungry ghost, or hell-being. Just as one's present physical condition is the result of deeds done in past lives, so the mental activities of the present motivate actions that shape the future. Shakyamuni Buddha said, 'To determine what you did in the past, examine your body. Examine your mind to discover what will come in the future.'

The cause of excellent resources within life as a human or a god is generosity; therefore, one should neither steal nor be

miserly but engage in charity. In order to be free from quarrel-
ing and situations of fright one should cultivate patience, and
to be able to discriminate the proper path from the false, one
should make great effort at study. One should cultivate meditative stabilization in order to free the mind from distraction and
should train in wisdom so that the true nature of phenomena
can be cognized. If in this life one engages in the six perfections,
the causes of happiness – giving, ethics, patience, effort, concentration, and wisdom – then their effect, happiness, will
definitely arise either in this lifetime or in the future.

Having heard in this way about practice of the path, one
should think about the cause and effect relationship between
the paths and their fruits, until conviction is generated. Then
meditation can be commenced. Nihilists, on the other hand,
say that meditation is senseless because it does not directly give
rise to physical comfort and prosperity in this lifetime. However, one will not always remain in this lifetime; all persons
definitely die. Since the longest condition of life is in future
lives, it would be senseless to cast aside the greater perspective for
the fleeting present. The time of death is indefinite, and when
it arrives, one cannot even take along one's body, not to consider relatives, friends, or wealth. Nothing helps except mental
predispositions accumulated from religious practice, for the
mind and its predispositions, which induce happiness and
suffering, travel together.

Meditation is the most powerful means of re-structuring the
mind, and cultivation of equanimity is an important initial
meditation. Let us discuss it.

The opposite of equanimity is desire and hatred, intimacy and
alienness. For instance, when a friend dies, one is worried and
cries because the person was very close and desirable. However,
when an alien or distant person dies, one is happy and takes
pleasure in his pain. Moreover, when a person neither de-
sirously close nor hatefully distant dies, one feels little and
thinks no more about it, not even worrying as much as when a
cup is broken. These reactions are the result of intimacy and
alienness.

If one does not abide in equanimity, believing that all beings – hell-beings, hungry ghosts, animals, humans, demi-gods, and gods – should be equally happy and free from suffering, pure religious practice and meditation cannot occur. In order to gain such equanimity, one meditates, reflecting that all living beings, even though they might not be intimate in this lifetime, were so in former births.

A story will illustrate this. The present Dalai Lama is the sixty-seventh incarnation of Avalokiteshvara, who has been appearing in the world since the time of Shakyamuni Buddha to help sentient beings. Among those incarnations were seven clairvoyant adepts, one of whom was wandering and came upon a family. As he approached, he saw a young woman cuddling her beloved child on her lap while eating a lamb chop. She set down the meat for a moment, and a dog came and took it away whereupon the mother threw a stone at the dog, almost killing it. When the adept viewed this with his clairvoyance, he saw that the mother's parents had had an enemy who had destroyed their household; he died and took rebirth as the child the woman held so lovingly. The mother's father had died and been reborn as the sheep whose flesh she was eating. Her mother had died and taken rebirth as the dog whom she had almost killed with a stone. The adept was saddened and sorrowfully thought, 'She cuddles on her lap the enemy who destroyed her family. She eats the flesh of her father and throws a stone at the head of her mother,' and he wept.

Since cyclic existence is beginningless, there is no sentient being who has not acted as a nurturing friend. Just as parents and friends in this lifetime have been kind, so all other beings have shown great kindness. Only through the fault of desire and hatred does one think that some are suitable for friendship and others fit only for hatred. In fact, in former lives all these persons, both the intimate and the alien, have been both one's enemies and one's friends. Even enemies sustained one in former lifetimes with loving care; therefore, all sentient beings should be recognized as kind mothers. Their appearance as foes now is due to being crazed by the afflictions of desire and hatred, much as if one's own mother had become temporarily insane.

Hence, the preliminary step in meditation is the development of a sense of equanimity free from desire and hatred toward all beings; one realizes their equality in having been in every possible relationship to oneself. Then, one can recognize them as mothers, the actual first step. The second step is to become mindful of the extent of their kindness when they were close, and the third is to develop an intention to repay their kindness, like a debt. The fourth is to develop love in the sense of finding pleasantness in everyone and responding with wishes for their happiness. The fifth step is compassion, the wish that all beings be free from suffering and its causes, and the sixth is the unusual attitude, the intention that one will join all with happiness and free them from suffering. The seventh and final step is altruistic mind generation, the development of a determination to attain Buddhahood in order to carry out this high resolve.

The seven cause and effect meditations begin with the preliminary step of equanimity because unbiased love and compassion are impossible without it. Let me illustrate this with a story. In the past in East India, a religious man went to his guru to receive precepts; he was told to go into retreat to cultivate patience. He did so, but when he finally left his retreat, someone said a rough word to him whereupon the practitioner answered bitterly and struck him. Other meditators heard of this and criticized him, saying that he had not meditated well. He laughed and said that he would meditate in a way that would exceed anything that any of them could do.

He resumed his retreat, intent on cultivating patience. A friend decided to test him to see if he actually had cultivated it. He defecated on a plate and carrying that plate behind his back, went to the practitioner's room and asked, 'What are you doing?'

'I am cultivating patience.'

'What kind are you cultivating?' his friend asked.

'A patience such that no matter what anyone says or does, I will not answer back.'

His friend said, 'Oh, in that case eat shit!' and suddenly put the plate down in front of him. The meditator picked up the plate and threw it back, saying, '*You* eat shit!'

After his friend left, the meditator was sad, reflecting that his friend must have been testing him to see if he was successful in his meditation. He was contrite and understood that he himself was at fault, whereupon he meditated with great effort and ultimately succeeded. To prevent such occurrences, he cultivated equanimity, recognizing that sentient beings have equally been both friend and enemy countless times.

Cultivation of equanimity begins the process of mental transformation culminating in *bodhichitta*, an altruistic aspiration to enlightenment. At that point one attains the first level of the Mahayana path of accumulation, the first of the five paths – accumulation, preparation, seeing, meditation, and no more learning. One is then a true Mahayanist and a Bodhisattva. Thus, generation of an aspiration to highest enlightenment for the sake of all sentient beings is the door to the Mahayana, just as refuge is the door to the proper practice of Buddhism in general. Equanimity prepares the ground for love and compassion which in turn induce this altruistic aspiration, the precious source of the qualities of Buddhahood.

The actual meditation of equanimity is cultivation of the thought:

> May all sentient beings abide in an equanimity free from intimacy and alienness, desire and hatred. May they not fight, considering some to be alien and others to be intimate. May they value everyone equally.

One should assume the sitting posture of the Buddha Vairochana, the adamantine (lotus) posture or half (lotus) posture. The eyes should be slightly open, directed at the point of the nose; otherwise, the mind will be distracted by objects of sight. The backbone must be straight, without bending forward, backward, to the right, or left. The shoulders must also be straight, and the head set naturally without arching back or bending forward but such that the nose is in line with the navel.

The lips and teeth should be set naturally, but with the point of the tongue at the ridge behind the upper teeth in order to decrease the flow of saliva.

The hands can be set in any of many fashions. One way, called the position of meditative equipoise, is to place the right hand on top of the left palm in the centre of the lap. Another, called the posture of meditative equipoise touching the earth, is to place the left hand flat on the lap with the palm upward and the right hand over the right knee touching the ground with the finger-tips. Another is the resting posture of Avalokiteshvara in which both palms are set flat on the ground at the sides; this affords relief for those who are cramped.

Breathing should be neither noisy nor constrained, but soft and gentle such that one cannot hear it oneself. To avoid distraction from seeing forms, hearing sounds, smelling odours, experiencing tastes, and feeling tangible objects, the breath should be counted until twenty-one, figuring each pair of breaths in and out as one. The mind will thereby be set one-pointedly without distraction. Refuge can then be taken:

> I go for refuge to the Lama.
> I go for refuge to the Buddha.
> I go for refuge to the Doctrine.
> I go for refuge to the Spiritual Community.

Then one-pointedly cultivate the thought:

> May all sentient beings abide in an equanimity free from intimacy and alienness, desire and hatred.

To do this, visualize a neutral person, one who is neither a friend nor an enemy, and think:

> This person was both friend and enemy countless times in the past. He wants to be happy and does not want to suffer but over the course of lifetimes has created the causes of suffering through conceiving some as intimate and helping them and others as distant and harming them. How nice it would be if both he and I could become free from desire and hatred, intimacy and alienness, and abide in equanimity!

Then imagine a pleasant being in front of you and think:

> Although he is pleasant now, he was my enemy in the past, and
> thus I should consider him equal with neutral beings. Except that
> now I like him due to the force of desire, he and the neutral
> person, whom I presently neither desire nor hate, are not at all
> different.

Then imagine an enemy and think:

> That I do not like this person now is due to his having harmed me
> in this lifetime; except for that, he, like the others, was my
> parent in the past and took care of me with kindness. Though my
> relatives and friends have acted nicely toward me in this lifetime,
> they harmed me in the past. Thus, they are all similar.

Through following this pattern of meditation over a long
period of time, considering first the neutral, then friends, and
then enemies, one can develop the thought of equanimity such
that a particular relationship of the moment will no longer
serve as a cause of desire or hatred.

At the end of each session of meditation, one should dedicate
its merit to the welfare of all beings:

> May the beneficial virtue of having meditated today serve as a
> cause of all beings abiding in equanimity.

A story from Shakyamuni Buddha's teaching illustrates how
dedication protects and maintains virtues. When Buddha was
residing in Bodhgaya, he told 2250 Hearers that anger destroys
the roots of virtue accumulated over many aeons, whereupon
the Hearers thought, 'There is not one among us who does not
become angry; thus, none of our virtuous roots have remained.
Even if we perform virtue, its force cannot be amassed. Since
we get angry many times every day, we are in a terrible
plight.'

When they related this to Buddha, he poured a little water
into a vessel and asked, 'Will this remain without evaporating?'
Because India is very hot, the Hearers thought, 'In a few days
the water will evaporate. This must mean that our virtue will
not remain at all,' and they became even more worried. Then

Buddha said, 'If this water is poured into the ocean, it will remain until the ocean itself evaporates.'

In the same way, if the virtue of a meditative session is dedicated to help and bring happiness to limitless sentient beings, then until that actually occurs, the virtue will not be lost. Furthermore, the benefit of hearing, thinking, and meditating within the motivation of seeking the welfare of all persons is as inconceivably vast as the number of beings in the many world-systems.

2 *Cyclic Existence*

Because Buddhist practices lead by stages to the state of a Foe Destroyer (*Arhan*) and eventually to Buddhahood, they are like roads for travelling and thus are called paths. The chief of these are the three principal paths: the intention definitely to leave cyclic existence, the aspiration to highest enlightenment for the sake of all sentient beings, and the correct view of emptiness.

The first is the decision to attain freedom from the bondage of cyclic existence – a state impelled by the force of actions and afflictions in which one is forced to assume a contaminated mind and body. Caught in the process of cyclic existence, one must then be born, grow old, become sick, and die again and again in the six types of migrations – hell-being, hungry ghost, animal, human, demi-god and god.

The afflictions of desire, hatred, and ignorance are the support of contaminated actions and thus are the final root of cyclic existence. All common beings powerlessly engage in actions through these three poisons, thereby accumulating the predispositions necessary to impel rebirth. For instance, due to liking food, drink, and resources one engages in many forms of lust. Through hatred one fights and kills. Obscured through ignorance, not knowing that one will be involved in non-virtue, one powerlessly accumulates the causes of future suffering; even if one does not wish to do so, due to the force of conditioning over beginningless aeons, one continuously engages in and thereby accumulates such actions. Upon amassing great non-virtue, one is born as a hell-being; from middling non-virtue, as a hungry ghost; and from small non-virtue, as an animal. Through amassing virtuous actions, one is born as a god, demi-god, or human.

There are eight hot, eight cold, trifling, and neighbouring hells, and among these let us use an example of rebirth in the first of the eight hot hells, called Reviving. When, due to a former action such as murder, one is born in the Reviving Hell, one immediately has a weapon in hand and is uncontrollably fighting others. The combatants slash and sever each other's limbs until all fall down unconscious; then, from the sky a voice issues forth, saying, 'Revive!' All are physically restored and renew the round of brutal attack. No matter how much one is mutilated, the cycle of attack, wounding, and revival continues until the lifespan, impelled by a former non-virtuous action, is exhausted.

Similarly, as a hungry ghost one is bereft of food, drink and resources, not finding in a year the nutriment that a human uses in a day. When one finally arrives at the shore of a lake, the water disappears or turns into undrinkable filth. When one finally finds food, it will not pass down the throat which is obstructed.

The sufferings of animals, such as stupidity, constant fear, and being used by others, do not require description just as the plight of humans – involving birth, ageing, sickness, death, meeting with the unwanted, losing the wanted, and so forth – is familiar to all. Demi-gods are particularly afflicted with jealousy of the prosperity of the gods and consequently engage in battle, thereby suffering wounds, losing limbs and even their lives. The gods superficially appear to have great happiness since they enjoy the desirable resources of pleasant forms, sounds, odours, tastes, and tangible objects for a very long time, but during the seven days preceding their death, they foresee their rebirth in a bad migration due to having spent their life in idle pleasure, reaping the fruit of previous virtue but not engaging in new virtue. The light of their body fades; their garlands wilt; their bodies smell; and the other gods avoid them.

Thus, though there might be a little happiness in cyclic existence, it gradually turns into suffering. One must develop the wish definitely to leave this state and attain a peace in which all suffering is extinguished. This can be understood through the four noble truths:

true sufferings
true origins of suffering
true cessations of suffering
true paths.

True sufferings are the contaminated mental and physical aggregates of hell-beings, hungry ghosts, animals, humans, demi-gods, and gods, which are generated through the force of contaminated actions and afflictions. These disintegrate moment by moment and thus are *impermanent*. Unable to remain for a second moment, they are *miserable*.

Impermanent and miserable, true sufferings are *empty* of being a permanent self or under the control of one. Also, they are *selfless* in the sense of not being a substantially existent or self-sufficient person or under the control of such a person. True sufferings have these four qualities – impermanence, misery, emptiness, and selflessness.

The causes of this repeated birth, ageing, sickness, and death must be determined if the disease is to be cured. The sources of suffering are the afflictions – mainly desire, hatred, and ignorance as well as anger, enmity, jealousy, laziness, and so forth – and actions contaminated by these afflictions. Without abandoning the basic causes, there is no way to overcome suffering; therefore, the afflictions are called the faults of all sentient beings throughout space that must be removed. To do this, one must attain true cessations which are conditions of the absence of the afflictions such that they will never return. To do this, true paths must be cultivated; one must generate the wisdom realizing emptiness which acts as an antidote to the misconception of inherent existence that serves as the support of afflicted states of mind, and then thoroughly cultivate this understanding in meditation.

B

To summarize the essence of the wish definitely to leave cyclic existence, one decides to forsake true sufferings and their sources and to attain true cessations and paths. To seek these for oneself furthers one's own welfare but does not pass beyond the path of a being of middling capacity. Rather, one should wish that all sentient beings, oneself and all others, emerge from cyclic existence; this is a path of a being of great capacity.

Merely hearing about such a practice establishes predispositions for the path of freedom. According to the Chittamatra system, predispositions are established on the mind basis of all (*ālayavijñāna*); then, later, when one meets with appropriate circumstances, these latencies provide the substance for generating the stages of the path.

According to the Svatantrika-Madhyamika system, there is a subtle mental consciousness that is the person who has travelled from life to life since beginningless cyclic existence. The predispositions or seeds for generating the capacity to free oneself from bondage are established on this subtle mental consciousness by hearing about the wish to leave cyclic existence. Similarly, in the Prasangika-Madhyamika system, potencies are established on the 'mere I', which is only imputed by thought and is reborn from life to life; then in the future – in this or another life – when one hears or thinks of this doctrine, these potencies are activated, providing the capacity for quickly generating the paths of liberation. An example will illustrate this: A man came before Buddha wanting to become a monk, and Buddha asked the Hearers if he was qualified. They answered that he did not have the merit to be a monk, whereupon the man became so distressed that he left to throw himself in a river. The Teacher called the man to him and said, 'The Hearers have said that you have no merit to become a monk, but in a former lifetime you took birth as a bug on top of an elephant's faeces in a pool surrounding a reliquary of a former Buddha. You have the merit of having circumambulated that reliquary.' Thus, if predispositions can be established from such an action, it is needless to say that they can be formed through hearing and contemplating doctrine.

The thought is:

I will free myself from misery and attain the peace of extinguishment. Then, having fulfilled my own aims, I will cause all beings throughout space to abandon suffering.

One should generate the thought until, like a prisoner about to be executed and seeking release from his plight, one decides definitely to free oneself and all others, attaining the peace of extinguishment and forsaking the afflictions that cause birth, ageing, sickness, and death again and again in the six migrations.

3 Altruism

If the intention to overcome the process of cyclic existence is not conjoined with altruism, one will attain only freedom from suffering, not the Buddhahood that is a perfection of one's own and others' welfare. Therefore, the altruistic aspiration, called the mind of enlightenment (*bodhichitta*) is most important.

Within Buddhism, those of the Hearer and the Solitary Realizer Vehicles cultivate the paths of a being of middling capacity – the thought to leave cyclic existence, together with the view of emptiness. Thereby they attain liberation, but due to not cultivating the altruistic mind of enlightenment they cannot attain Buddhahood. The mind of enlightenment, in general, is of two types, conventional and ultimate, and the conventional is again divided into the aspirational and the practical.

The aspirational mind of enlightenment is the wish to attain Buddhahood in order to help all sentient beings; it marks the beginning of a Bodhisattva's accumulation of meritorious power in conjunction with wisdom and continues until Buddhahood, having twenty-one forms called 'earth-like', 'gold-like', and so forth, which are instances of its increasing in strength as one progresses. The practical mind of enlightenment occurs when, having taken the Bodhisattva vow, one actually practises the six perfections of giving, ethics, patience, effort, concentration, and wisdom. The ultimate mind of enlightenment is a wisdom consciousness in meditative equipoise directly cognizing emptiness attained at the time of the Mahayana path of seeing.

To become a Bodhisattva one must cultivate the conventional mind of enlightenment, specifically in its aspirational form. As was explained before, it involves seven steps in the system transmitted from Buddha to Maitreya to Asanga:

1 recognition of all sentient beings as mothers
2 becoming mindful of their kindness
3 intending to repay their kindness
4 love
5 compassion
6 unusual attitude
7 altruistic mind generation.

Having practised equanimity and reflected on the plight of cyclic existence in the two previous meditations, one is prepared for the first step, recognizing all persons as mothers.

This meditation is to visualize individually every sentient being that one has known, beginning with recent friends, then passing to neutral persons, and then to enemies, identifying each as having been one's mother. One should meditate until everyone, from bugs on up, is understood as having been one's mother. Since this is the door to generating the mind of enlightenment, its benefit has no boundary or measure as will become apparent in meditation.

The next step is to cultivate mindfulness of the mothers' kindness, first with respect to friends, then neutral persons, and then enemies. The essence of the practice is to become aware that even if persons are now enemies, neutral, or friends, they have in the past been as kind as one's own mother of this life.

What is the kindness of a mother? First of all, one enters her womb while she copulates with a mate. At that time one's mind has entered into the soft substance of the father's semen and the mother's blood. During the second week the fetus becomes a little hard, like yoghurt; in the third week, it becomes -oundish, and during the succeeding weeks bumps appear that develop into limbs – head, arms, and legs. Then, while one's body grows by stages over many weeks, one undergoes indescribable discomfort due to the way the mother lies, eats, and so forth, and she also suffers great physical and mental discomfort as one's body forms. Still, she considers the child more important than even her own body; fearing that her child might be harmed, she makes great effort at proper diet, habits of sleep, and activity.

When about to be reborn, the baby turns around inside the womb and begins to emerge, causing the mother such pain that she almost swoons. Though finally her vagina is torn, her body harmed, and she has undergone great suffering, she does not throw one away like faeces, but cherishes and takes care of her child. Her kindness is greater than the endearment she has for her own life.

One should also reflect on the delightful ways a mother holds a baby to her flesh, giving her milk. She must provide everything; she cannot tell the baby to do this or that; she must attentively do everything herself. Except for having the shape of a human, the child is like a helpless bug. She teaches it each word one by one, how to eat, sleep, put on clothes, urinate, and defecate. If one's mother had not taught these, one would still be like a bug. Even when a cat gives birth to a kitten, one can directly see that the cat undergoes great hardship to take care of the kitten until it is able to go on its own.

Just as one's present mother extended great kindness, so those who now are enemies were mothers in former lives and extended the same kindness, and in later lifetimes they will again protect one with kindness. If it were necessary to become angry when it is determined that someone is an enemy, then since one's present parents and dearest friends were enemies in a former lifetime and will be in the future, it would be necessary to hate them. But if one's mother became incensed and attacked oneself, would it be right to become angry and beat her, or would one try to calm her and restore her mind to its usual state? In the same way, an enemy is only one's own best friend who has lost control and, without independence, is attacking oneself. He is not at fault; he is not acting under his own power. He has helped before and will help again. When one was inside his womb, how much suffering he underwent! After one was born, how many difficulties he had to bear!

The thought is:

> Each and every being, upon taking birth in cyclic existence over the beginningless continuum of lives, has protected me with kindness, just like my mother in this lifetime, and will do so again in the future. Their kindness is immeasurable.

When, having considered friends, neutral persons, and enemies, one is clearly mindful of their kindness, one should cultivate the third step, developing the intent to repay their kindness:

> I will engage in the means to cause all to have happiness and to be free from suffering. Just as they helped me in the past, now I must help them.

One should alternate analytical meditation – analysing the reasons for repaying the kindness of others – and stabilizing meditation – fixing on the meaning understood – finally gaining a measure of the kindness of each and every being throughout space and developing a sense of the need to respond.

4 Love and Compassion

The fourth of the seven cause and effect precepts is love. The field of observation is all sentient beings, and the subjective aspects are three:

1 How nice it would be if all sentient beings had happiness and its causes.
2 May all sentient beings have happiness and its causes.
3 I will cause all sentient beings to have happiness and its causes.

These are three levels of increasing strength which should be cultivated gradually until the point of spontaneity is reached.

The *King of Meditations Sutra* (*Samādhirāja*) says that the benefit of cultivating love with all sentient beings as the field of observation is immeasurably greater than that of offering to Buddhas and Bodhisattvas over many aeons even lands filled with food, drink, and articles. The *Sutra on Manjushri's Buddha Land* (*Mañjushrībuddhakshetra*) says that there is a Buddha Land to the north-east of this world where beings have attained cessation of coarse feelings and discriminations, abiding most comfortably in meditative stabilization without suffering. Being so happy, they find it easy to behave purely, not killing, stealing, engaging in sexual misconduct, and so forth, for many thousands of ten millions of years. The sutra says that although the benefit of their practice is great, it is more beneficial to cultivate love here for the time it takes to snap the fingers.

One should first take as the object of observation a friend

and cultivate the wish that this person have happiness. When this becomes easy, one should consider a neutral person and cultivate the wish as before. Then, one should consider an enemy and cultivate love until there is no difference between the wish for happiness that one has for the friend, the neutral person, and the enemy. The meditation should be extended slowly to all sentient beings throughout space, reflecting again and again on the disadvantages of not having and the advantages of having happiness. One may then gradually ascend through the three subjective aspects.

Even if one meditates only once for only five minutes taking cognizance of all sentient beings and even if the love consciousness, due to unfamiliarity, is weak, the virtue is inconceivable because the scope is so vast. For example, if a sesame seed is squeezed, only a little oil comes out, but if many are squeezed, a barrel can be filled with the oil.

Initially, the meditation should not be longer than fifteen minutes in order to avoid fatigue and retain enthusiasm. Later, it can be lengthened until immeasurable love, conjoined with meditative equipoise, is eventually attained. When love is cultivated little by little, very clearly, with all beings as the field of observation, it is as if one is repaying in part the immeasurable kindness that others extended in former lifetimes.

The next step is to cultivate compassion. The field of observation of a compassionate mind is all sentient beings who have any of the three types of suffering – of pain, of change, and of being so composed as to be always ready to undergo pain.

The suffering of pain is actual physical or mental discomfort included in which are birth, ageing, sickness, and death. Many billions of years have passed since this world was formed; many have been born here, but there is no one who has managed just to stay alive. It is necessary to die and take rebirth again and again.

Sufferings of change are feelings of pleasure which, when superficially considered, seem to be pleasurable but can change into suffering. For example, if a person is out in the sun where it is too hot, he is pleased to go to a cooler spot, but if he stays there too long, he will become cold and sick. Similarly, when one becomes too cold and then goes to a hot place, if one gets too hot, one will fall sick. Although there is a seeming pleasure in becoming cooler or warmer, if one stays in that state too long, it turns into suffering. This shows that these situations do not have an inherent nature of pleasure.

Similarly, in this world beings – whether animal or human – mate with pleasure, but if it is not done in a moderate amount, the pleasure is lost. Excessive copulation can cause a disease called 'cold and wind' in the lower abdomen, harming both male and female genitals. Though enjoyable at first, it can ruin the very basis of comfort in the vital channels (*nāḍī*). Thus, these feelings of pleasure are said to be contaminated and are called sufferings of change.

The third type of suffering is called that of pervasive composition. Whenever a sentient being takes birth by the power of contaminated actions and afflictions in the desire, form, or formless realms, there are periods when he does not have manifest suffering. However, if certain conditions aggregate, suffering will be generated because the basic causes of misery pervade all types of life within the three realms. For instance, though one might have no manifest suffering now, if one is pricked with a needle, cut with a knife, or kicked, pain is immediately produced.

The field of observation for a compassionate mind is all sentient beings who have these three types of suffering; however, to understand the suffering of others, it is necessary first to know the immeasurable fault of one's own birth in cyclic existence. One should think:

> I have engaged in non-virtue since beginningless time and have accumulated bad actions *(karma)*. I suffer pain and change. I am afflicted by being always liable to suffer pain.

One should contemplate the causes of suffering – the ten non-virtues, how one has engaged in them, and how one has suffered in this lifetime. There are three physical, four verbal, and three mental non-virtues.

PHYSICAL NON-VIRTUES

1 *Killing:* taking the life of a human or any other being. If one has committed murder, one is born in a bad migration, and then when that migration is finished, even if one is reborn as a human, the lifespan will be very short.

2 *Stealing:* taking what is not given. Through its force one will have few resources in the future, and whatever one has others will steal.

3 *Sexual misconduct:* incest, copulation in the presence of an image that is an object of refuge, or with a woman about to give birth, and so forth. Such misconduct leads to being controlled by desire and hatred in the future.

VERBAL NON-VIRTUES

4 *Lying:* saying that what is is not, that what one does not have one has, or the opposite. From such deception one will not hear the truth in the future.

5 *Divisiveness:* creating dissension between people or increasing dissension that already exists. The fruit of dividing people is that one will not have friends and will hear oneself frequently faulted by others.

6 *Harsh speech:* speaking from anger in order to harm. For instance, when directing someone to go here or there, one does not speak politely but says, 'Can't you get over here?!' The effect is that one will be reborn in a place where one must always be scolded.

7 *Senseless talk:* conversation not about religious practice, the affairs of one's family or country, but about meaningless subjects. Through wasting one's life unconscientiously in meaningless talk one will not hear sensible talk in the future and will be reduced to speaking gibberish.

MENTAL NON-VIRTUES

8 *Covetousness:* the desire for acquisition upon seeing the property of another person. This causes poverty and leads to losing whatever property one has.

9 *Harmful intent:* the wish to injure another, male, female, animal, and so forth. Based on this deed, people will not be agreeable in the future.

10 *Wrong views:* asserting that the cause and effect of actions do not exist, that the Three Jewels are not sources of refuge, and the like. If due to such views one perversely holds that there is no fault in engaging in the three physical or four verbal non-virtues, this harms the roots of virtue already formed in one's mental continuum and thereby induces great suffering in the future.

One should gradually call to mind one's own non-virtues and reflect on the cause and effect process that induces suffering. It is appropriate to generate contrition, a sense of discomfort with former misdeeds, and a promise to refrain from those deeds henceforth.

Reflection on one's own involvement in the causes of suffering ultimately generates an intention to leave cyclic existence. One comes to know that just as one has suffered in this lifetime, after death the process will begin again and wherever one is born – even as a god or a human, one must suffer. Having formed a clear sense of one's own situation, one should then consider a friend:

> This person has the three types of suffering and is also engaging in the causes of further misery. Even when he finishes undergoing the suffering of this lifetime, he will have more in the next. How nice if he were free from suffering and its causes! May he become so! I will cause him to become so!

Then one should consider a neutral person and after that an enemy. Gradually and over a long period of time, one can slowly extend the meditation to all sentient beings.

Having developed facility first with respect to a friend, such as one's mother, one is able to measure the progress with respect to neutral persons and enemies by comparing it to the strong feeling for the friend. Why should one make all neutral persons and enemies equal to one's mother? If she had fallen into a ravine or a river, or into a chasm made by an earthquake, and if her own child whom she had helped from the time of his entry into her womb would not help her, who would?

5 Assuming the Burden

The sixth of the seven cause and effect precepts for generating a mind of enlightenment is the unusual attitude, which involves cultivation of love and compassion with special force. The mere wishes, 'How nice it would be,' or 'May they have these,' are no longer sufficient; one should think:

> Alone I assume the burden of causing all sentient beings to have happiness and the causes of happiness. Alone I assume the burden of causing all sentient beings to be free from suffering and its causes. Being a child of all these beings, if I do not try to make them happy, I will be shameless.

One is the child who was helped by each and every sentient being, and it is as if those beings – one's parents – have fallen into a river or a ravine, and broken their legs. Considering them this way, one should take upon oneself the task of making them happy and freeing them from suffering.

The mind willing to assume this burden is called the unusual attitude of love and compassion; it should be cultivated not only in meditative session but also afterwards when going, standing still, eating, working, or lying down. Even though one might be working, in the depths of the mind the force of the thought, 'I will cause all beings to be free from suffering and joined with happiness,' must remain indestructibly.

Continuous cultivation is needed; for example, if the bitter bark of a tree is mixed with a few drops of molasses or a little sugar, the bitterness will not be relieved, but if it is soaked in either, it will. In the same way, mere occasional cultivation of love and compassion will not become the unusual attitude; one must meditate frequently over a long time. The mark of having generated this high resolve is that in all modes of behaviour this assumption of the burden of others' welfare remains inseparably with the mind. Then, one is no longer just *practising* the paths of a being of great capacity but *is* such a being – having abandoned one's own aims and become intent upon the welfare of others.

Even if Hearers and Solitary Realizers reach the end of their paths and become Foe Destroyers, they are still only beings of middling capacity; they must train in recognition of all persons as their mothers, becoming mindful of their kindness, intent on repaying their kindness, and developing love, compassion, and the unusual attitude. When they generate the latter, they become beings of great capacity and are called 'those who formerly generated the realization of a Foe Destroyer'.

Persons who have generated the unusual attitude need to know how sentient beings can be freed from suffering and made happy; otherwise, their meditation will be only a wish. Upon investigation they discover that only those who have the status of a blessed Buddha can actually bring vast benefit to others. They have passed beyond the faith of clear delight, which is simple delight in the qualities of a Buddha, and have attained the faith of conviction. They understand that Shakyamuni Buddha originally generated an aspiration to highest enlightenment, accumulated the collections of merit and wisdom for three countless aeons, and finally became fully and perfectly enlightened into the body, speech, mind, qualities, and activities of a Buddha, and they understand that by their following this path the same result will be produced. Having come to believe that there is great purpose in attaining Buddhahood, they generate the third type of faith, the wish to attain the state of a Buddha – one who has abandoned all faults and has attained all realizations. They have examined their condition and have seen that now, never mind helping others, they cannot free even themselves from misery. Thus, they ascertain with valid cognition the necessity of attaining Buddhahood and then examine their minds to determine whether such attainment is possible. Through careful study of emptiness, they see that the mind is not naturally defiled with desire, hatred, and ignorance, that these are peripheral factors, whereas the nature of the mind is intrinsically pure. They thereby ascertain with valid cognition the capacity to attain Buddhahood.

Such persons have taken upon themselves the burden of the welfare of all sentient beings and have seen that they must and can attain Buddhahood. They arrive at the last of the cause and effect precepts: the promise to attain Buddhahood. This is the altruistic aspiration to highest enlightenment. As Maitreya's *Ornament for the Realizations (Abhisamayālaṃkāra)* says, 'The mind of enlightenment is the wish for complete perfect enlightenment for the sake of others'. It is the thought:

> I will attain complete perfect Buddhahood in order to free all sentient beings from suffering and cause them to be happy.

In all the scriptures and their commentaries, there is no more helpful meditation. Even merely understanding the presentation of this meditation is said to be of such great benefit that if one attempted to enumerate it, one would not finish for many thousands of aeons.

The circumstances for hearing such teaching are rare, but it is clear in Buddha's word that there are many in the West who will generate this altruistic aspiration, seeking to aid others. In his 100,000-stanza and 25,000-stanza *Perfection of Wisdom Sutras (Prajñāpāramitā)* Buddha made a prophecy: 'In the future, and then in the future, it will spread to countries in the North. Then, it will spread here. Two thousand five hundred years after my death, the excellent doctrine will spread to the land of the red-faced people.' This refers to the spread of the Buddhist teaching to Tibet and then to Mongolia, during which time it disappeared in India. Then, it returned to India, 'here', when the Tibetans fled their country in 1959 and established many monasteries in India. Thus, in between times, the teaching spread back to India, and now it is being carried to the Americas, the land of the red-faced people, the home of the red Indians. The dissemination of Buddhism to the West began in 1957, 2500 years after Buddha died.

Hearing about the three principal paths to highest enlightenment is rare and occurs only through one's merit; thus, one should not leave it as an object of hearing but engage in meditation. If a meditator's mind is strong and if the object – the field of observation – is special, then the effect of the meditation is experienced in the present life. If not very strong or special, the effect is experienced in the next life. When one does not think forcefully about the field of observation but just meditates, 'May they be free from suffering and the causes of suffering', this is an uncertain action, it not being specifiable when the effect will mature. Therefore, it is important to petition the Three Jewels for help and enthusiastically extend the scope of altruistic wishes to all beings.

6 Wisdom

The cause behind sentient beings' uncontrolled travelling in cyclic existence is misconception of the nature of objects. Thus, realization of the correct view – unmistaken cognition of the mode of being of all phenomena – is central to achieving liberation. Among the several ways of asserting the correct view in the higher and lower schools of Buddhist tenets, I will explain here the final system, Prasangika-Madhyamika.

A false nature of things appears to the mind and, not knowing this to be false, beings assent to it and thereby are drawn into afflictions that necessitate wandering in cyclic existence. Therefore, it is said that whatever Shakyamuni Buddha and the earlier Buddhas taught was for the sake of realizing emptiness. They taught emptiness directly to those who were vessels of direct teaching, and if a student was not suitable for such explicit teaching, they taught practices conducive to realizing emptiness. They did so in order that beings might abandon obstructions, liberating themselves from cyclic existence and attaining Buddhahood. Thus, in the commentaries on Buddha's word it is said that if a person forms an understanding of the correct view, then Buddha's purpose in coming to the world is fulfilled. Those who generate the thought definitely to leave cyclic existence and the altruistic aspiration to highest enlightenment do indeed fulfil Buddha's purpose, but not as do those who realize emptiness in conjunction with the other two paths. This is because the wisdom that realizes the emptiness of inherent existence is like a mother giving birth to the auspicious attainments in Hinayana and Mahayana, allowing abandonment of obstructions and attainment of the fruits of both vehicles.

Wisdom is the mother, and method – the motivation of seeking to leave cyclic existence or to attain highest enlightenment for the sake of all sentient beings – is the father. If one does not have the wisdom realizing emptiness, it is impossible to abandon the obstructions to liberation, as Hinayanists seek to do. Similarly, without it one cannot abandon the obstructions to omniscience and obtain Buddhahood, as Mahayanists seek to do. In Tibet, Mongolia, and so forth, when a mother has husbands of different countries and gives birth to a son by each, the sons receive the names of their fathers' lineage. In the same way the correct view is like a mother in that it is shared by all vehicles and is necessary for their attainments, while the different methods of the vehicles are like fathers, in dependence on which the differences in lineage and attainment arise.

Motivated by the wish to free oneself from the sufferings of cyclic existence and attain liberation, a Hinayanist meditates on emptiness and eventually attains the state of a Foe Destroyer. Motivated by the wish to attain highest enlightenment for the sake of all sentient beings, a Mahayanist cultivates this same correct view in order to abandon the obstructions to omniscience and by combining method and wisdom eventually attains Buddhahood. The mother, the correct view, is common to the vehicles in that it is utterly impossible to abandon the obstructions to their respective attainments without it.

Even if understanding of emptiness does not form and one only generates the suspicion that persons and other phenomena *might* be empty of inherent existence, the predispositions that cause rebirth in cyclic existence are torn to shreds. Aryadeva explains in the *Four Hundred (Chatuḥshataka)* that if one generates the altruistic aspiration, thinking, 'I will attain Buddhahood for the sake of freeing all sentient beings from cyclic existence,' then, as explained before, the benefit is as great as the limitless number of sentient beings throughout space. Similarly, even if the correct view has not been realized, when one conjoins the altruistic aspiration with an intention to train in wisdom, Aryadeva says that the benefit is sixteen times greater than cultivating the altruistic aspiration alone. The thought is:

> I will generate the correct view and eradicate all suffering in order that all sentient beings may attain Buddhahood.

The many ways for generating the correct view are condensed into four essentials, through which emptiness can easily appear to the mind. The first essential is to identify the object negated in the theory of selflessness – the opposite of emptiness, inherent existence. In the selflessness of persons this is the appearance of 'I' as if it exists in and of itself, as if it exists by way of its own nature and entity.

If the 'I' inherently existed, it would not just be designated to mind and body but would exist under its own power, in its own right. If the 'I' did exist in its own right, then when sought, it would be findable. Is the head 'I'? Are the arms 'I'? Are the hands 'I'? Are the fingers 'I'? Are the legs 'I'? No.

For example, usually when we see the body of a cow, we think that it is the cow itself, whereas actually the body of a cow is the basis of the designation 'cow' and is not a cow. The feelings of a cow, such as its being hot, cold, comfortable, or miserable, are not a cow; they are only feelings. The discriminations of a cow, such as 'This is tasty', 'This is bad', 'This is liquid', 'This is grass to be eaten', and so forth, are not a cow; they are just discriminations. Similarly, the mind of a cow such as in thinking, 'I should go over there', or 'This is my calf; I should lick it', is not a cow.

In the same way, a human is only designated to the collection of these five aggregates – forms, feelings, discriminations, compositional factors, and consciousnesses. A person is only imputed in dependence on the mental and physical aggregates; the aggregates together or individually are not the person. Under analysis, the 'I' cannot be found.

However, in some Buddhist systems, each of the five aggregates is asserted to be the person, and in others the mind alone is said to be the person, such as the Chittamatra assertion that the mind basis of all is the person and the Svatantrika position that a subtle mental consciousness is the person. The fact of the matter is that individually the five aggregates are not the person and neither is their composite. Though when one sees the body of a cow, one thinks, 'This is a cow,' that body is not a cow. When its meat is eaten, the cow is not eaten, but its flesh is. The composite of the physical and mental aggregates is the basis of the designation of the name 'cow'. After having performed such analysis, when the body of a cow is seen, one will understand that this functions as seeing a cow but will not feel that the body of a cow is a cow.

Similarly, the mental and physical aggregates of a human are the basis of the designation 'human' but are not a human. However, when ordinary persons view their own mental and physical aggregates, they continually think, 'I, I', with the sense that it naturally exists, that it can even be pointed to with a finger. This thought of 'I' is called the innate misconception of 'I'; without study or training, persons have engaged in it since beginningless cyclic existence.

When an emptiness of inherent existence is realized and when this realization is supplemented with the cultivation of love, compassion, and the altruistic aspiration, then on the first Bodhisattva ground one can easily give away one's body if asked, without feeling pain. In the past, Shariputra – one of the two supreme persons who are frequently depicted on either side of Buddha – generated an altruistic aspiration to highest enlightenment for the sake of all sentient beings. At a time when he had not directly realized emptiness, a demon came near him while he was cultivating compassion in meditation, and thought, 'He is about to attain Buddhahood; I must destroy him.' So he approached Shariputra and said, 'I am making offerings and need a human hand.

Please give me one of your hands,' and he cried and bowed down.

Because Shariputra was a Bodhisattva and even though he had not directly realized emptiness, he thought, 'This is suitable,' cut off one hand, and gave it to him. It hurt Shariputra a great deal, but he thought that it had helped the man and returned to his meditation whereupon the demon saw that Shariputra's meditation had become even stronger.

He again approached and beseeched him, 'I made a mistake about the hand. I do not need that hand; I need the other one. Please give it to me.'

Shariputra allowed him to cut it off, and returning to meditation, he thought, 'I gave one hand; now, I have given the other. How terrible the pain! Through this I can see how much suffering there must be for beings born in hells. How unbearable it must be!'

Thus, his cultivation of compassion again increased whereupon the demon was again disgusted; he cried and hit his head on the ground, shouting, 'He has done such a terrible thing to me!'

Shariputra looked at him and thought, 'I cut off my right hand and gave it to him, but he was not pleased; so, I gave him my left hand, and yet he carries on like this. If I cannot help even one sentient being through giving my own body to him, how could I possibly help all? I will not be a Bodhisattva.' Thus, Shariputra fell back to the level of a Hinayana Hearer. What was at fault?

He had not realized the emptiness of inherent existence of his body and was ruined through his own misconception of its nature. If he had attained a union of calm abiding and special insight realizing the emptiness of inherent existence, then his understanding would have increased when giving his body, and he would have been able to use the pain which he still had, due to not having cognized emptiness directly, to increase his compassion for sentient beings stricken with severe physical suffering. He would never have fallen.

This is because calm abiding is an ability of the mind to fix on an object as long as one wishes, and special insight is an investigation into the nature of phenomena. When a union of these two is attained, then there is no concern about suffering from mutilating the body; otherwise, when the body is mutilated, one's attitude can become worse, even causing one to forsake the intention to help others.

On the first Bodhisattva ground, emptiness is realized directly, and a surpassing perfection of giving is attained, at which time it is possible to give away anything without either worry or hope for reward. When one thoroughly sees that the mental and physical aggregates do not exist under their own power but through the force of contaminated actions and afflictions, they are known as only a means of assuming the suffering of birth, ageing, sickness, and death, not as a source of goodness. If another needs them, one can give them without regret.

Meditation on emptiness means to meditate on non-inherent existence or the inability of phenomena to establish themselves. Since emptiness is a negation of the object negated, which in relation to a person is the inherent existence of that person, the first step in the process is to identify the sense of a self-established, self-powered, inherently existent 'I' or person, not just nominally imputed, but existing in its own right. It is important to seek help from the Three Jewels in furthering the meditation, thereby establishing predispositions which, even if they do not ripen into an actual realization in this lifetime, will do so quickly in the future. The thought is:

> O Buddhas residing in the ten directions, please help me to realize emptiness. Please help me to identify the object negated in the theory of selflessness.

With a subtle portion of mind, one should watch the sense of 'I' as if from a corner, without overpowering the main consciousness such that the sense of a concretely existent 'I' disappears. An incident can be remembered in which one was falsely accused and there was a clear sense of the 'I' who was falsely accused, or one can remember being helped by another and at that time having a clear sense of the 'I' who was helped. One should cultivate this sense of 'I', watch it, and see what it is like. Without a clear sense of the inherent existence that is negated is the theory of selflessness, talk about emptiness and meditation on it are like shooting an arrow without knowing where the target is.

7 Nagarjuna

After the first three of the thousand Buddhas of this aeon had come, our Teacher Shakyamuni was born to King Shuddho-dana and Queen Maya. Shakyamuni resided in the capital of the kingdom until he was twenty-nine, during which time he married, fathered a child, and having completed the study of politics, was appointed king in his father's place, enjoying the privileges of royalty. However, at the age of twenty-nine he left the householder life, and for six years, until the fifteenth day of the fourth month of his thirty-fifth year, he practised asceticism. Then, we say, he 'showed the manner' of becoming a Buddha, because according to the Prasangika-Madhyamika system, he had attained Buddhahood aeons ago and was only showing the way in which Buddhahood is attained.

For seven days he remained silent, but when Brahma, king of the gods, beseeched him to teach, he turned the first wheel of doctrine on the four noble truths at Varanasi on the fourth day of the sixth month. Living until his eighty-first year, he turned three such wheels, setting forth 84,000 bundles of teaching. Before passing away on the fifteenth day of the fourth month of his eighty-first year Buddha said, that he had ripened those trainees whom he could ripen and that the time of his staying in manifest form as a Buddha had passed. He advised all to practise.

According to the Prasangika system, Buddha's appearance in this world system and his passing away merely occurred to the

sight of ordinary trainees for the sake of showing them how to
practise. He did not newly become enlightened here but had
become so many aeons ago and came to our world system as a
superior Emanation Body. After one is enlightened, there is
no need to die; it is only to common sight that one does. He
thought that if he stayed on and on, his followers would not
practise diligently. Near the time of his death, the Hearers,
Foe Destroyers, and Bodhisattvas, such as Manjushri and
Vajrapani, gathered and asked Buddha a question, 'When you
die, who will bear and spread your system?'

Buddha said, 'Four hundred years after I pass from sorrow, a
monk named Shriman will be born in Vidarbha in South
India. He will be also called "Naga". Without error he will
spread the greatest among the many doctrines of Mahayana.
In the common view, he will be a first ground Bodhisattva, and
afterwards he will go to the Blissful Pure Land.'

In accordance with this prophecy, Nagarjuna, the disseminator of the Madhyamika system, was born in South India
four hundred years after Buddha's passing away. It is said that
he lived six hundred years, his life being divided into three
proclamations of doctrine; during the first, he became a monk
at Nalanda, and later, as prefect, he corrected the wayward
discipline of many monks. Nalanda was a monastery as great as
a large town, with 40,000 resident monks; much later when the
Muslims invaded India, they destroyed it as completely as the
Chinese have destroyed the large monastic centres in Tibet.
Near the end of the first proclamation, when Nagarjuna was
lecturing to the 40,000 monks, he saw two strangers, who
looked like humans, at a distance. When the monks dispersed,
he went to where they had been standing and perceived a
fragrant smell. At a subsequent lecture, he saw that they were
carrying incense in their hands, and he told the monks that
they should bring the two strangers to him.

They came, carrying their incense, and when he asked, 'Where
do you come from? What is that incense?' they said, 'We are
Nagas. When we stay with humans, their strong smell affects
us badly. Thus, we carry this incense to prevent contagion.'

'Where is your country?'

'It is at a great distance. Please come there. We have books from the earlier Buddhas, Krakucchanda, Kanakamuni, and Kashyapa, and also from the teacher of this era, Shakyamuni Buddha, such as the *One Hundred Thousand Stanza Perfection of Wisdom Sutra (Shatasāhasrikāprajñāpāramitā)*. When turbulent times came to the Mahayana, these books were taken to our land. We will take you there.'

Nagarjuna said, 'From among the many *Perfection of Wisdom Sutras* we do not know the version in one hundred thousand stanzas. Do you actually have it?'

'Yes, indeed.' Thus, Nagarjuna decided to go to Nagaland where he saw the images and books of former Buddhas and the extensive, middling, and condensed *Perfection of Wisdom Sutras* of Shakyamuni. He taught the Nagas, who offered him the *One Hundred Thousand Stanza Perfection of Wisdom Sutra* which he brought back to India.

In his absence, many people wondered where the protector Nagarjuna was, and thus even nowadays some feel that there must have been a second Nagarjuna. Actually, his return was his second appearance in that region and marks the beginning of his second proclamation of doctrine. During this period he composed the *Six Collections of Reasoning,* establishing emptiness as the final mode of existence of all phenomena and thereby founding the Madhyamika (Middle Way) system.

Later Nagarjuna went to the Northern Continent and again returned to India, appearing there for a third time – the first being his birth and the second his return from Nagaland. This time he brought back the four scriptures that serve as the basis of Maitreya's explanation in his *Ornament for the Mahayana Sutras (Mahāyānasūtrālaṃkāra)*.

After almost 600 years, he went to reside near the King Shatavahana to whom he had earlier sent his *Precious Garland of Advice for the King (Rājaparikathāratnāvalī)* and his *Friendly Letter (Suhṛllekha)*. The queen had not allowed their son to engage in the usual princely studies because the king had a karmic relationship with Nagarjuna whereby he would live as long as Nagarjuna; thus, the queen thought their son would never become king. Several of the boy's friends told him, 'If you do not start studying the royal duties, you will never be able to assume the throne.'

The boy was very upset and asked his mother many times why he was not being trained, but she just said, 'That's all right; don't worry about it.' Finally he became angry, saying to his mother, 'I must become king. I am a prince, your child. If I do not study, I cannot take care of the kingdom.' She then explained to him his father's relationship with Nagarjuna.

Later, he told his friends, who were all of royal lineage, the reason. In time they all went to Nagarjuna, bowed down, and begged him to die. Again and again they beseeched him, 'Our royal lineage will be ruined. Please die. Let him become king.' Nagarjuna had attained many special powers and thus was able to live a very long time, but because they requested him so often, he wondered what he could do. Thinking over his past lives, he remembered cutting the back of a worm with a blade of *kusha* grass; so, he told the prince to bring a blade of *kusha* grass, with which the boy was able to cut off Nagarjuna's head. The members of the royal lineage rejoiced at Nagarjuna's death, and it is said that from that time the monarchies in India began to weaken.

During his second proclamation of doctrine, Nagarjuna established the Madhyamika system, which also relies on the books of his students, Aryadeva and Chandrakırti, as well as those of Shantideva. The basic text of Madhyamika is Nagarjuna's *Treatise on the Middle Way (Madhyamakashāstra)*, to which Buddhapalita composed a commentary that Bhavaviveka refuted. In turn, Chandrakirti refuted Bhavaviveka, supporting Buddhapalita, and thereby clarified the Prasangika system as the true meaning of Nagarjuna's thought. Bhavaviveka was very learned, but in his Svatantrika system, he explained that even though phenomena are empty of true existence, they conventionally exist in their own right, whereas in Prasangika, if something exists in its own right, it necessarily truly exists. From this viewpoint Bhavaviveka's system is not final.

If phenomena existed in their own right, they would not be dependent-arisings; they would not depend on causes and conditions or even on their own parts for their existence. Such phenomena as here and there, the near and far banks of a river, and you and I exist only in relation to their respective places of dependence. On this side of the river, this is the near bank, but on that side, the other side is the near bank. It is the same with east, west, south, and north; none of these exist under their own power or in their own right; they rely on definite causes for their designation; they are dependent-arisings.

The reason for striving in meditation to realize dependent-arising and emptiness is that all problems – birth, ageing, sickness, death, fighting, discomfort when it is hot or cold, hunger, and pain – arise from the afflictions, which depend on ignorance of the nature of phenomena. This is the root of travelling in cyclic existence, and if one is able to destroy it, one can create happiness; otherwise, even if progress is made, it is like winning one war but having to fight another. In order to stop the process of cyclic existence and the arising of the unwanted, one must destroy ignorance, the view of the transitory mind and body as an inherently existent 'I' and inherently existent 'mine'.

The view of the transitory mind and body as a real 'I' is the conception of *oneself* as inherently existent, whereas the conception of another as inherently existent is a conception of a self of persons but not 'a view of the transitory collection as a real "I" '. Similarly, the view of the transitory collection as inherently existent 'mine' is the view that *one's own* head, body, or mind, for instance, inherently exist. When these misconceptions of 'I' and 'mine' are stopped, the process that generates the suffering of cyclic existence is overcome.

How do persons conceive themselves to exist inherently? The bases of the designation 'I' are forms, feelings, discriminations, compositional factors, and consciousnesses which are called the five aggregates; the 'I', or the person, is the phenomenon designated to these aggregates. The 'I' and the aggregates nominally or conventionally are one entity; however, ordinary persons do not conceive the 'I' to exist nominally or conventionally. Rather, the 'I' is conceived to exist in its own right.

If the 'I' and the mind and body exist in their own right, then they must be either the same or different. If anything under consideration exists, it will be either one or different. Without a decision that these two are the only possibilities, Madhyamika reasoning would be inconclusive. Car and house are different, and car and car are one, whereas this car and that car are different. There is no third category beyond same and different. Though an innate consciousness mistakenly assuming inherent existence does not conceive the 'I' either to be one with or different from mind and body, *if* the 'I' existed in such a solid way as it is conceived by this innate wrong view, then it would have to be either the same as or different from mind and body.

In the previous meditation one determined the object negated in the theory of selflessness – an inherently existent 'I' – but now one should analyse the conditions that would have to be true if the 'I' existed in this way. The purpose of these investigations is to overcome the ignorance that causes all the suffering of cyclic existence; thus, it is important to ask for help in the meditation:

> I will cultivate the view that the 'I' does not exist in its own right, that it is only imputed there by thought. I petition the Three Jewels for help in developing the realization that if the 'I' inherently existed as it appears to do, it would be either one with mind and body or a different entity completely.

Snow Lion Publications

P.O. Box 6483
Ithaca, New York 14851

Snow Lion Publications

Our periodic mailings are an excellent way to learn of new publications as they are released. Please fill in your name and address below (or the name of an interested friend or book dealer). Just add postage and drop it in the mail. You'll be hearing from us......

Name _____

Street Address _____

City _____ State _____ Zip _____

8 Are a Person and Mind and Body the Same or Different?

In the first step of meditation on selflessness, one identifies a person that inherently or naturally exists, exists in its own right, truly and actually exists, exists covering its bases of designation, or in and of itself without depending on thought. These are called *hypothetical* synonyms of self because in fact the person does not exist in these ways at all. If the 'I' inherently existed, it would not depend on causes and conditions or even on its own bases of designation; it would exist under its own power. Thus, in the second step one reflects on the fact that if the person did exist the way it appears, then it would have to be either one with mind and body or a different entity from them.

This is because mind, body, and a person exist, and there must be something to point to for each of them, if they *concretely* exist. For instance, if the person were one with the mind, then when one 'points' to the mind – or has a clear sense of mind as a concrete entity – one is pointing to the person. Or, if the person were one with the body or a part of the body, then when one points to that, one is pointing to the person. If the person were a different entity from mind and body, then one could point to the mind and body over here and to the person over there, not necessarily in a different place, but at least susceptible to being pointed out separately.

If the person exists the way it appears, so forcefully, so concretely, as if it existed in its own right, it should become clearer and clearer when one searches for it. Thus, in the second step of meditation on selflessness one determines that if the person exists the way it appears, it must be findable either as mind and body or as a different entity. The third and fourth steps are to consider these two possibilities.

First, let us consider whether mind and body, which are the bases of the designation 'I', and the 'I', which is the object designated, are one. If the person were the same as mind and body, then since mind and body are two, the person would be two, or since the person is one, then mind and body would be one.

In another way, consider the five aggregates – forms, feelings, discriminations, compositional factors, and consciousnesses. If the person were one with these, then since these are five, the person would be five. Or, since the person is one, the aggregates would absurdly be one.

Through this type of reasoning, enlarging it according to one's knowledge, one should come to a firm decision that the mental and physical aggregates and the 'I' are not one. Then, if the 'I' inherently exists, the only other possibility, is that it differs from mind and body. The 'I' would then be apprehendable separately from mind and body. In meditation one should clear away all instances of mind and body – the aggregates of forms, feelings, discriminations, compositional factors, and consciousnesses – and see if the 'I' that originally appeared to have its own basis, its own inner nature, is apprehendable without mind and body. When sought, it will not be found anywhere; thus, the 'I' is not only not mind and body but also not separate from mind and body.

To do this meditation one must patiently search many months for the 'I', using as a guide one's innate sense of 'I' and then applying reasoning. Through repeated investigation, a stronger and stronger sense of the unfindability of a concrete 'I' will gradually develop; a vacuity will appear, not one of nothingness, but a negation of concrete, inherent existence.

Does this vacuity contradict dependent-arising? Not at all. Dependent-arising and emptiness are compatible; dependent-arising itself is a sign that phenomena do not exist in their own right. For instance, barley, rice, and cabbage grow in dependence on causes and conditions; they do not appear through their own nature. An effect depends upon its causes for its production, and a cause also depends upon its effect because independently it could not be called a cause.

Self depends on other, and other on self; they do not exist under their own power, or in their own right. The same applies to the far and near banks of a river, to tall and short, high and low, male and female. None exist naturally.

All phenomena depend on causes and conditions, on other phenomena, or on their own parts for their existence. There is no phenomenon that is designated independently. This is the great reasoning of dependent-arising, the mode of establishment, the mode of being of phenomena. If one does not realize this and instead apprehends phenomena as if they exist under their own power, then this misapprehension of the nature of objects acts as the cause of wandering in cyclic existence.

This misapprehension is of two types, artificial and innate. Artificial misconceptions of the nature of phenomena derive from belief in wrong systems of tenets, in dependence on which the false appearance of concrete existence is explicitly affirmed through citing reasoning and scripture. The innate misconception of the nature of phenomena is inborn, existing from beginningless cyclic existence, without study or reasoned affirmation. Beings in cyclic existence unanalytically assent to the false mode of appearance of things as if they concretely exist, assuming their appearance to be true.

As an easy example, we can consider the misapprehension of permanence, which is a manifest misconception of the nature of things such that, no matter how long we have lived, we still plan to do such and such tomorrow, this the next day, that the day after, this the next year, and on and on. We do not exactly think, 'I am permanent; I will not die', but act as if our basis were permanent. Usually we only think about clothing, possessions, and activities, planning the various stages in which

c

they will be used. This mode of apprehension accords with a conception of permanence.

There are indeed cases of babies dying in the womb or shortly after birth, or children dying in their youth before their parents, but our thought is that we will last forever. Similarly, when meeting someone whom we last saw six years ago, we think that we are meeting just that same person, without realizing that he has changed.

In the same way, our innate sense of inherent existence misconceives the nature of 'I' without explicitly using words like 'inherently existing in its own right', or 'naturally existing'. Also, just as when we examine and discover the impermanence of persons and things, we see them differently and no longer make plans with a sense that we will never die, so when we examine and discover the non-inherent existence of persons, we experience ourselves and others differently. We discover that this concrete sense of 'I' is baseless.

Is the 'I' the head? Is it the body? Is it the stomach? Feelings? Discriminations? Compositional factors? Mind? It is none of these, being only designated to them. Many cannot accept an 'I' that is merely designated in dependence on mental and physical aggregates but cannot be found among the aggregates. They feel that this would be nihilism; they cannot comprehend the compatibility of analytical unfindability and dependent-arising, which to them seem contradictory. They think that whatever is a dependent-arising must be analytically findable. Therefore, the Chittamatrins and Svatantrikas teach that when one searches to find the person, one finally discovers a subtle consciousness that passes from lifetime to lifetime and is the 'I'.

For the Chittamatrins who follow Asanga, this is called the mind basis of all. For the Chittamatrins who follow Dharmakirti and for the Svatantrikas, this is a subtle form of the mental consciousness. They know that the person is not the eye, ear, nose, tongue, or body consciousnesses, for these are just the basis of designation of the temporary 'I'. They see that the body is taken to the funeral pyre or cemetery at death and does not continue to the next life; thus, they conclude that the mind is the person. They cannot comprehend how rebirth and the cause and effect of actions could be possible when the person only imputedly exists.

These are examples of artificial or intellectually acquired conceptions of the inherent existence of 'I'. The basic thought in these systems is that when the object considered is sought – such as a person or a table, which are imputed to mind and body and to the parts of a table – they are found, either as one among the many bases of designation, as in the case of a person, or as the composite of the bases of designation, as in the case of a table. These schools hold that the table is the collection of four legs and a top whereas the Prasangikas assert that the collection of the parts is only the basis of the designation 'table' and not a table. If the mind were the person and since persons are male and female, are there male and female minds? Do minds have male and female genitals? Does a mind have eyes?

In the Prasangika system the person is the 'I' imputed in dependence on the collection of mental and physical aggregates. This imputedly existent 'I' is misconceived to exist inherently, as if it were concrete and findable. Based on this misconception of the nature of things, from beginningless cyclic existence until now, sentient beings have been accumulating virtues and non-virtues, some being born as hell-beings, others as hungry ghosts or animals, and others as humans or gods. Not considering persons and phenomena to be merely dependently imputed, beings ascribe independence to persons and phenomena and through this misconception of the status of things are forced to take birth in a condition of suffering.

The conception of inherent existence is not abandoned through merely withdrawing the mind from such a thought but through losing belief in inherently existent objects. This is why one considers whether the 'I' is the same as or different from mind and body. Through analysing these two with reasoning over a long period of time, one can lose belief in a concrete, findable 'I' because if it cannot be found among mind and body or separate from mind and body, where can it be?

The conception of inherent existence is just like the conception of permanence – baseless.

Beings have been afflicted with this misconception since beginningless cyclic existence; therefore, a mere superficial understanding of non-inherent existence is not sufficient. The realization must be cultivated until emptiness appears clearly. Not only will long cultivation of this in meditation free oneself from cyclic existence, but also it will, when conjoined with altruism, confer the ability to free other sentient beings from suffering. Therefore, as a means to enhance the process of meditation it is helpful in general to petition the Three Jewels and in particular Manjushri, who is the physical manifestation of the wisdom of all Buddhas in the ten directions just as Avalokiteshvara is of their compassion and Vajrapani is of their power.

The new attainment of wisdom by Bodhisattvas, their training in the high qualities of the path, realization of emptiness, proceeding to Buddhahood, and subsequent accomplishment of others' welfare are achieved in dependence on Manjushri, the father of all Conquerors. Shakyamuni Buddha, all Buddhas in the past, and those of the future did and will expand their intelligence and attain Buddhahood in dependence on Manjushri. Thus, for those who want to further their intelligence in this and future lives and to understand the correct view, the means is the recitation of Manjushri's mantra:

> Homage to the lama and the protector Manjushri, undifferentiable. Oṃ a ra pa tsa na di ['phonetically', om a ra ba dza na di].

The mantra should be recited a hundred, twenty-one, or at least seven times. On the last repetition, repeat the final 'di' as much as possible.

In the past, the Mongolians living in Russia, Outer Mongolia, and Inner Mongolia were extremely skilled in the Buddhist treatises due to having been taught as students to recite this mantra when having difficulty understanding a topic. Here the topic is the nature of phenomena. One should think:

Despite the fact that from beginningless cyclic existence I have been apprehending myself to exist inherently, I do not exist inherently. In order to help all sentient beings throughout space, I am entering into meditation analysing whether the 'I' and its bases of designation, mind and body, are one or different entities.

Manjushri's mantra may be recited at this point, after which one should reflect on the reasoning why the 'I' cannot be inherently one with or different from mind and body. Through concluding that such a concrete 'I' does not exist, the 'I' will be viewed as a dependent-arising, arising through designation in dependence on mind and body.

9 Nothingness is Not Emptiness

In the past, after Buddha's teaching had spread to Tibet, a degenerate form of Buddhism was propagated there by a Chinese monk called Mahayana Ho Shang. Shantirakshita, an important early Indian disseminator of Buddhism to Tibet, prophesied the need to call on his student Kamalashila to debate with Ho Shang. The reason was that the Chinese abbot would spread a method of meditating on emptiness wherein the meditator was not to think about anything. Ho Shang's view was that cause and effect and so forth do not exist, not non-exist, not both exist and non-exist, and not neither exist nor non-exist. His technique was to sit comfortably without thinking of anything. 'Just as a white cloud blocks the sun, so does a dark one,' he said, meaning that both virtue and non-virtue obstruct realization of the unfabricated suchness of phenomena. He had sources for his teaching from sutra, but he did not know their proper application in the stages of the path.

Kamalashila, author of the three *Stages of Meditation (Bhā-vanākrama)*, was invited to Tibet according to Shantirakshita's word, debated with Ho Shang (approximately 792 AD), and defeated him, restoring Buddha's own system in the land of snowy Tibet. The conditions of the debate were such that when the Chinese monk lost, he had to leave the country – the system of the victor being adopted by the country as a whole. He left, taking all of his belongings except one shoe. From this Kamalashila drew the conclusion that although it had been shown that

Ho Shang's teaching did not accord with Shakyamuni Buddha's actual system, a little of his method of meditation would remain. Thus, even though Buddha's teaching thrived, Ho Shang's system of meditation on emptiness remained in scattered places throughout Tibet and China.

However, not thinking about anything and meditation on emptiness are contradictory. For ordinary persons, if an understanding of emptiness has not been conceptually formed, it is impossible to meditate on emptiness. It is necessary to distinguish between the manifest mode of meditation on emptiness of a Superior and the non-manifest mode of a non-Superior. The former is a direct realization of suchness in which the wisdom consciousness cognizing emptiness and emptiness itself are like fresh water poured into fresh water, undifferentiable. It is called the space-like meditative equipoise. For those who have not attained the path of a Superior, however, emptiness appears in a non-manifest manner; this means that a generic image of emptiness appears to thought when an understanding has formed. For example, one can call to mind a mental image of a person who is not present. Through a generic image of emptiness an inferential consciousness realizes an absence of inherent existence until, by accustoming to this absence through the medium of an image, a yogic direct perception is attained in which emptiness is seen as if with the eyes.

Prior to that time, however, one must form an *understanding* of emptiness or selflessness of which there are two types, of persons and of other phenomena. The emptiness of a person is a person's non-inherent or non-true existence. The emptiness of phenomena refers to the non-inherent or non-true existence of phenomena other than persons, their analytical unfindability.

Primary among these phenomena are the six constituents – earth, water, fire, wind, space, and consciousness, which are the bases of the designation of a person. The earth element refers not just to common earth but to the hard substances in the body, such as bone, hair, fingernail, skin, and so forth. Water similarly refers to the liquid elements of the body, blood, pus, urine, and so forth. Fire does not mean mere fire, but the warmth of the body. Wind refers to the five types of currents: vitalizing, pervasive, downwards-voiding, upward-moving, and heat-accompanying winds. When these four elements and their potencies are in balance, the body is healthy whereas when they are imbalanced, disease sets in. For instance, when the earth element predominates, it is difficult to move, rise, and so forth. When the water element predominates, water accumulates in the legs and other parts of the body. When the fire element predominates, one suffers fever and its attendant maladies. When the wind element predominates, one becomes excited and anxious. However, when the elements are balanced, it is easy to move back and forth, to maintain an equal temperature, and to remain balanced mentally.

The space constituent is not the non-product space – the mere absence of obstructive contact – but the holes and empty places in the body, the passageways of the gullet, intestines, and so forth. The consciousness constituent is composed of the six minds – eye, ear, nose, tongue, body, and mental consciousnesses, among which the latter is chief.

One should carefully identify these constituents in one's own continuum; they are the bases of the designation of a person but are not a person. In the Prasangika system, even the mind is a basis of the designation 'person' and not itself a person. Otherwise, there would be many persons.

Taking these six constituents as a basis, one can meditate on their being empty of existence in their own right. If one is practising the Mahayana motivation, one meditates not just to free oneself from cyclic existence but mainly to attain highest enlightenment in order to establish each and every sentient being throughout space in Buddhahood. By meditating on emptiness, opposing the false mode of apprehension of phenomena, one will realize that the conception of inherent existence is a perverse consciousness and will gradually develop a realization of the truth that is capable of acting as an antidote to misconception, thereby opening the way to full enlightenment.

As before, one should meditate on the non-inherent existence of the six constituents through analysis of whether they are the same as or different from their bases of designation. Initially, one should ascertain a clear notion of the inherent existence of earth, water, fire, wind, space, or consciousness within one's continuum. For instance, one could identify the appearance of a concrete, findable skeleton and then identify the basis of the designation 'skeleton', a collection of many bones arranged in a certain shape. Or, one could examine a moment of consciousness, the bases of designation of which are the beginning, middle, and end of a moment.

Then, one should reflect that if the phenomenon designated and the basis of designation inherently and concretely exist as they appear to do, they must be either the same or different. Is the skeleton the same as each of the bones? No, because then each person would have many skeletons or there would be just one bone. Is a moment of consciousness the same as the beginning of the moment, the middle, or the end? If so, there would be three moments, or there would not be three parts.

Once it is firmly decided that they are not the same, one should analyse whether the phenomenon designated is different from the basis of designation. One can imaginatively remove all bones to see whether a separate skeleton can be found. The beginning, middle, and end of a moment of consciousness can be removed to see whether a separate moment of consciousness can be found. One can then understand that skeleton and moment of consciousness do not exist in the concrete way that they seem to.

One should not state these reasons merely for the sake of making a superficial decision. First, the target was erected – one's own sense of a concrete object on which desire and hatred are based; thus. the aim of such fourfold analysis is to realize and abide in a consciousness realizing that phenomena have no objective base, even though they appear to be so solid. One should come to disbelieve these false appearances, like a magician watching his own creations but not believing in them. Eventually one will understand that skeleton and moment of consciousness are dependent-arisings; a skeleton arises in dependence on bones, and a moment of consciousness on the beginning, middle, and end of a moment.

In this context 'arise' does not mean 'produce' but 'exist'. A skeleton exists, designated in dependence on a collection of bones, as does a moment of consciousness, designated in dependence on the beginning, middle, and end of a moment. In this way, emptiness and dependent-arising are compatible; an understanding of the one helps that of the other. Far from being a negation of phenomena in general, emptiness refers to a specific absence of a falsely conceived solid nature in things. Through becoming accustomed to it in the space-like meditative equipoise, both the conception that assents to the false appearance and the false appearance itself will gradually be overcome, yielding the magnificent qualities of a Buddha. Though emptiness is a mere negative of inherent existence, its realization, when conjoined with love and compassion, allows the spontaneity of a Buddha's activities of altruism.

10 Summary: The Supreme Practitioner

Persons whose capacity is small aim at not being reborn in the next life as a hell-being, hungry ghost, or animal and seek rebirth in a happy migration as a human or god. Persons of middling capacity aim at attaining the happiness of freedom from cyclic existence, whereas those of great capacity aim at establishing all sentient beings in the state of Buddhahood. All practitioners and practices can be included in these three basic types.

During the second dissemination of Buddhist doctrine in Tibet the Indian pandit Atisha (982–1054) was invited there where he taught the practices of beings of small, middling, and great capacity. Several Tibetans came to him and asked, 'If we practise for the sake of happiness in this lifetime, is there not any benefit?'

Atisha answered, 'If you practise for the sake of only this life, the eventual effect is rebirth in a hell or as a hungry ghost or animal.' He was thinking that one's virtue would be uselessly spent in pleasures during this life, whereupon rebirth would be taken by the power of non-virtuous actions. Therefore, when hearing, thinking, or meditating, a practitioner's motivation should be directed toward something deeper than this life alone.

Death is definite though the time of death is indefinite; there is no one who has managed just to stay alive. At the longest one can live a hundred or so years; then the warmth collects from the extremities of the body, the outer and inner breaths cease, and consciousness departs. If one is to be reborn in a bad migration, the upper extremities become cold first, and one leaves through an opening in the lower part of the body. If one is to be reborn in a happy migration, the lower extremities become cold first, and one leaves through an opening in the upper part of the body.

At the time of death nothing helps except former practice, the door to which is refuge. The refuge of a being of great capacity is preceded by two causes; the first is concern for all sentient beings' cyclic existence, solitary peace, obstructions to liberation, and obstructions to omniscience. Cyclic existence is repeated birth, ageing, sickness, and death in the six migrations. Solitary peace is the mere bliss of the extinction of suffering without perfecting oneself in order to help other sentient beings. The obstructions to liberation are the conception of inherent existence and the desire, hatred, and obscuration so induced. The obstructions to omniscience are, firstly, the false appearance of phenomena as if they inherently exist whereas they do not and, secondly, the inability to cognize emptiness and the phenomena qualified by emptiness directly and simultaneously.

A being of great capacity is concerned about these four faults in all beings and believes that the Three Jewels – Buddha, his Doctrine, and the Spiritual Community – have the power to protect all from these faults. Concern over the four faults and belief that the Three Jewels have the power to protect from these are the two causes preceding the refuge of a being of great capacity.

Just as refuge is the door to Buddhist practice in general, so altruistic mind generation is the door to Mahayana practice. A being of great capacity realizes his own plight in cyclic existence and extends this understanding to all beings throughout space, seeing that it is also not suitable for others to undergo suffering. He thinks:

Though there can be great enjoyment in this lifetime, upon death nothing can help except practice. At that time I must leave all my property, gold, silver, and so forth; I cannot take my own relatives and friends with me. Nevermind that, I cannot even take my own body. Leaving all these, I must go alone. In the same way each and every sentient being throughout space must go alone. I must free myself from cyclic existence, but even if I did, all others would still have this great fault.

Instead of settling in the path of a being of middling capacity, he cultivates the path of a being of great capacity:

Even my enemies are merely enemies in this lifetime; in a former life they were my parents and like my present parents were extremely kind to me. Even if they act like enemies now, in the future they will be my parents and will extend great kindness and protection to me. My own mother, father, family, and friends of this lifetime are indeed very kind to me, but when I consider the kindness of all persons over the span of lives, they are all equally kind. It would not be suitable if they were unhappy and not free from suffering.

This is how a person proceeds on the path to becoming a being of great capacity. Like a prisoner to be executed in only a few days, he seeks liberation from the miserable condition of cyclic existence. Then, applying this understanding of suffering to all sentient beings and realizing the equality of all beings, he generates an equanimity that is free from desire and hatred toward friends, enemies, and neutral persons.

Having done this, he does not remain in a neutrality of ignorance, deserting and abandoning others, but realizes that each and every sentient being was his own mother in a former life and will be his mother in future lives. He reflects on their kindness:

They were extremely kind. First, I was formed in their wombs and emerged like a bug. They fed, nourished, and clothed me and taught me how to talk, walk, eat, study, and live. If I did not have them as parents, I would not have known how to talk; I would have remained like an animal although I looked like a human.

Even when he sees a bug, he thinks:

> Although having now taken the form of a bug, this person was
> my mother in a former lifetime and was extremely kind.

Then, he generates the intention to repay their kindness, the
love wishing sentient beings to have happiness and its causes
and the compassion wishing sentient beings to be free from
suffering and its causes.

When cultivating the unusual attitude, he thinks:

> I take upon myself the burden of joining all beings throughout
> space – as illustrated by my own parents – with happiness and the
> causes of happiness and freeing beings from suffering and the
> causes of suffering. I cannot do this now, and thus I must attain
> Buddhahood in order to do so.

This is the generation of an altruistic mind of enlightenment:

> It would not be right if I did not develop the power to help all
> sentient beings to be happy and free from suffering; therefore, I
> will attain Buddhahood. Once I have attained it, I will draw them
> all to Buddhahood.

With this as his motivation he engages in meditation cultivating
the correct view, realizing the nature of all phenomena,
persons and all else.

Such teaching is very rare in the world nowadays. Almost
entirely lost in Asia, it is no longer found in China or Tibet,
remaining only a little in Japan and again in India, where it has
been brought back by the Tibetan refugees. To derive its great
benefit, one needs to cultivate this thought in persistent
meditation:

> In order to establish all sentient beings – enemies, friends, and
> neutral persons – in the bliss of Buddhahood, I will engage in
> hearing, thinking, and meditating and attain enlightenment.
> Once I have become a Buddha, I will help all others to achieve the
> same. In order to do this, I will cultivate the three principal paths:
> the thought definitely to leave cyclic existence, the altruistic
> aspiration to highest enlightenment for the sake of all sentient

beings, and the correct view of emptiness, the mode of being of all phenomena.

If the benefit of such meditation had form, it would not fit into the world system.

Although it is necessary to take care of the present life, it should not be one's main activity; it will disappear very soon. As Shakyamuni Buddha said:

> Buddhas neither wash sins away with water, nor remove the sufferings of beings with their hands. They transfer not their realizations to others. Beings are freed through the teaching of truth, the nature of things.

Buddhas do not clear away suffering with their hands nor do they wash away non-virtues with water; they cannot pour the realizations which are in their own continuums into others. They liberate beings only through teaching the paths of freedom, what to adopt and what to discard, what is beneficial and what is harmful. Liberation depends on one's own practice.

PART TWO

Way of Compassion

A translation of Tsong-ka-pa's *Illumination of the Thought, an Extensive Explanation of Chandrakirti's 'Supplement to the Middle Way'*, chapters one to five.

In Praise of Compassion

A Preface to Tsong-ka-pa's
*Illumination of the Thought of Chandrakirti's 'Supplement to the
Middle Way'*

BY JEFFREY HOPKINS

*Homage to that compassion for migrators who are
Powerless like a bucket travelling in a well
Through initially adhering to a self, an 'I',
And then generating attachment for things, 'This is mine.'
[Homage to that compassion for] migrators
Seen as evanescent and empty of inherent
Existence like a moon in rippling water.*

These lines appear in the third and fourth stanzas of Chandra-kirti's *Madhyamakāvatāra*, which is perhaps best translated as the *Supplement to the Middle Way*. The Sanskrit *madhya* means 'middle', *madhyama* being 'the very middle', and the *ka* of *madhyamaka*, according to Bhavaviveka, is derived from the Sanskrit root meaning 'proclaim'. Thus, Jam-yang-shay-ba's textbook on Chandrakirti's *Supplement to the Middle Way* says that the root *ka* of *madhyamaka* in general refers either to a book that proclaims the system of the middle way, or to the tenets of that system, or to a person who teaches it. The *Madhyamaka* of *Madhyamakāvatāra* is said to refer to a text propounding the middle way, specifically Nagarjuna's *Treatise on the Middle Way (Madhyamakashāstra)*.

According to the Tibetan commentarial tradition, *avatāra* means 'addition' in the sense that Chandrakirti's text is a supplement that was historically necessary in order to clarify the meaning of Nagarjuna's *Treatise on the Middle Way*. It was necessary to make clear that Nagarjuna's *Treatise* should not be interpreted according to the Chittamatra (Mind-Only) system, or according to the other branch of Madhyamika, the Svatantrika, founded by Bhavaviveka. During Nagarjuna's lifetime, Bhavaviveka had not written his commentary to the *Treatise*, nor had he founded his system; therefore, it was necessary later to supplement Nagarjuna's text to show why it should not be interpreted in such a way.

Moreover, Chandrakirti sought to show that a follower of Nagarjuna should ascend the ten grounds by practising the vast paths necessary to do so. This is because some people interpret Madhyamika as nihilism. They see it as a means of refuting the general existence of phenomena rather than just their inherent existence – objective or natural existence – and conclude that it is not necessary to practise things such as the cultivation of compassion. Therefore, in order to show that it is important to engage in the three practices of common beings – compassion, non-dual understanding, and the altruistic mind of enlightenment – Chandrakirti, at the beginning of his *Supplement to the Middle Way*, pays homage to compassion:

> *Hearers and middling realizers of suchness*
> *Are born from the Kings of Subduers.*
> *Buddhas are born from Bodhisattvas.*
> *The mind of compassion, non-dual understanding,*
> *And the altruistic mind of enlightenment*
> *Are the causes of Children of Conquerors.*

> *Mercy alone is seen as the seed*
> *Of a Conqueror's rich harvest,*
> *As water for development, and as*
> *Ripening in a state of long enjoyment,*
> *Therefore at the start I praise compassion.*

Chandrakirti pays homage to compassion because it is the chief distinguishing feature of a Bodhisattva. Since Bodhisattvas are the causes of Buddhas, by paying homage to their main practice, he implicitly honours Buddhas who arise from this practice. He pays respect to the causes of Buddhahood because if one wants to become a Buddha, one must generate compassion and enter the Bodhisattva path.

Tsong-ka-pa, in his *Illumination of the Thought of Chandra-kirti's 'Supplement'*, implies that this obeisance to compassion is not merely a clever metaphor to attract people's attention, like the prattling of a parrot, for if it were, it would be senseless. Rather, it indicates stages of practice. Chandrakirti pays homage to three types of compassion: those which observe sentient beings, phenomena, and the unapprehendable. In Tsong-ka-pa's commentary, their meaning is particularly clear, so let us consider the first, compassion observing only sentient beings, in its light.

In the third stanza, quoted at the beginning above, Chandra-kirti gives the example of a bucket in a well, not merely as a clever way of describing the suffering of cyclic existence, but to provide a source of reflection so that practitioners can generate compassion. It is easy for a bucket to descend into a well but, once filled with water, very hard to rise again. As the bucket drops, it hits against the stones on the sides, damaging itself. Also, the windlass requires someone to turn it continually.

The wandering of the bucket from the top to the bottom of the well is the wandering of sentient beings in cyclic existence due to the force of the afflictions – desire, hatred, and ignorance – and the actions that are motivated by these afflictions. The turner of the windlass is an untamed mind. The top of the well represents the realms of gods, demigods, and humans, and the bottom the realms of animals, hungry ghosts, and hell-beings. It is easy to descend from a good to a bad migration and hard to rise from a bad migration to a good one. In other words, our minds are so imbued with the afflictions of desire, hatred, and ignorance that we naturally, like a bucket falling in a well, will be led to a lower level or migration; or, if we are already in a low one, we will remain there. As is said in scripture, those who die and go from a happy migration to be reborn in another happy one are as few as the grains of sand on the tip of a fingernail, whereas those in either a happy or a bad migration who are reborn in a bad one are as numerous as the grains of sand throughout the whole world.

A meditator has to imagine vividly that a bucket, as it easily descends, clanks against the side of the well and is scratched, bumped, and torn. It then takes great effort for the turner of the windlass to raise the bucket. In the same way, it takes effort for any sentient being, even though battered through the force of his own actions, to turn the mind, heavy with the afflictions of desire, hatred, and ignorance, toward virtue.

Whereas Chandrakirti had said in the first stanza that compassion is necessary, here in the third stanza he explains *how* to generate compassion in thoughtful meditation. Kensur Lekden, in explaining this stanza, made noises such as, 'Clang! Clang! Dr, dr, dr, dr, dr.' His kindness in frequently portraying the situation of the buckets was great; it came to the point where one vividly imagined the buckets being thrown here and there; one could no longer sit passively in front of him. One would even wince as he made the sounds of the clatter and rip. Since this situation is to be applied to sentient beings whose lives are like the example, the vividness of the example aids in stimulating compassion.

The first type of compassion is called 'compassion observing only sentient beings'. The word 'only' does not imply, as some commentators say, that the meditator necessarily observes *permanent* sentient beings just because they are not seen as qualified by momentary impermanence. Here, sentient beings are qualified only by suffering – wandering in the various types of cyclic existence like a bucket in a well.

Furthermore, Tsong-ka-pa says that it is not sufficient merely to reflect on how sentient beings suffer because if one reflects on the suffering of an enemy, one will be happy. One would think, 'Oh, I did not realize how much he is suffering. How nice it is!' Or, if someone to whom one is neutral is suffering, one would just disregard it, like reading in the newspaper that a person whom one does not know has been taken to a hospital in serious condition. However, when a person to whom one is close becomes ill, one is greatly moved; due to this closeness the sense of compassion, love, and concern is intense. Therefore, Tsong-ka-pa says that to generate unbiased compassion it is necessary to develop this same closeness and intimacy with regard to each and every sentient being. This has to be *cultivated* in frequent meditation simply because we do not now have a sense of closeness with our enemies. A realization of intimacy with all others will not remove the possibility of someone's acting as an enemy, but that fact will no longer be used as a reason for his being found distant and thereby suitable to be hated.

It is necessary to overcome the inertia of a mind filled with the afflictions of desire, hatred, and ignorance by reflecting on a means to view each and every person as being as close as one's dearest friend. This is called love in the sense of pleasantness; in other words, no matter how a sentient being looks externally, one finds him attractive. It is usually easy to feel love and compassion for a pleasant person, but an ugly or harmful person should also be valued in the same way.

There are two means for doing this. One, which stems from Maitreya through Asanga, is the sevenfold cause and effect precept for the generation of an altruistic aspiration to highest enlightenment. It begins with reflecting that each and every person has been one's mother. The purpose of identifying others in this way is that the mother is the greatest of friends; however, if one's mother is not so seen, one is advised, in the meantime, to choose someone else. Otherwise, when one made everyone equal to one's mother, one would extend the same ill feeling toward them. Still, it is a great key to choose the mother as the model of the closest friend, and it is necessary eventually to take her as the object. If we cannot rekindle our experience as a little child running up to our mother and holding on to her for protection and love, if we cannot restimulate the warmth for her, how could we possibly feel intensely for other people?

Upon reflection, it is due to our mothers that we are able to meet with the doctrine and with qualified teachers, and to hear a teaching that is helpful not just superficially or temporarily, but throughout the continuum of lifetimes. The effect of practice dedicated to the welfare of others will not diminish over the course of our lives. Would it have been possible to meet with such a precious source of help and happiness if our mother had left us, had abandoned us along the way, even for a day? We would have died. Or, as Kensur Lekden said, we would be like bugs, not knowing how to eat, talk, or walk. All these activities are dependent on her.

Against this, some think, 'It was by her own desire that I was born. She ought to take care of me.' Such an attitude is prevalent nowadays, and nothing could be more non-Buddhist. By her acting out her desire she provided a place where we could be reborn in a good migration. Therefore, it is our fortune that she happened to engage in the act at the time when we were looking for a place to take rebirth.

Since cyclic existence is beginningless, each person at some time has been in every possible relationship with everyone else; therefore, each has been everyone else's mother. Pabong-ka says that we need to reflect on their kindness to the point that when we see a bug crawling on the floor, we will reflect, 'In a former lifetime I was carried in the womb by this person!' If one has a child or has watched another care for a child, one knows how much attention must be given to it.

By recognizing other sentient beings as having been very intimate, kind and close, one naturally finds them to be pleasant, regardless of how they look or behave; a pleasantness is found in every sentient being. Without this, no matter how effective one is in cultivating a sense of sentient beings' suffering, compassion will not be generated.

The second means of generating compassion and the altruistic mind of enlightenment is the system transmitted from Manjushri to Shantideva, known as the equalizing and switching of self and other. Attempting to value and to view other beings as equal to oneself, one thinks, 'I am only one. Like all sentient beings I want happiness and not suffering. In this sense we are all equal. Because I am only one, and others are many, they are to be valued even more than myself.'

'Self and other' are very unusual. There seem to be two – self and other – and this self seems to be equal in number to other, whereas everyone else is 'self' or 'I' from their own point of view and oneself is other. When you say to me, 'You', I generally but not always interpret it as 'I'. Everyone is both 'I' and 'you' in certain senses, but even from my own point of view 'I' is not equal in number to 'other'.

Furthermore, as the Dalai Lama said in lectures on the stages of the path in 1972, if Buddha achieved enlightenment for the sake of all sentient beings, then he achieved it for all of us, and in this sense everyone is equal. A Bodhisattva does not think, 'So and so is attractive; I want to achieve enlightenment for him or her.' The altruistic aspiration is for the sake of everyone equally.

Others are also a field of merit. If one has a very fertile field, one values it and strives to take care of it; one looks at it with fondness even if it is covered with manure. In a similar way, each and every sentient being is a field by means of which one can develop the meritorious powers of love, compassion, and wisdom. Others are, therefore, far more important than oneself, and from this, one can learn to cherish others far more than oneself.

The second type of compassion is that which 'observes phenomena'. As Tsong-ka-pa makes clear, this means 'compassion observing sentient beings who are only designated to phenomena'. 'Phenomena' here refer to mind and body, the five mental and physical aggregates. Sentient beings are only designated to these; they do not have an entity independent or separate from the aggregates. Thus, it comes to mean 'compassion observing sentient beings who are qualified by being impermanent and empty of a substantially existent or self-sufficient entity.'

Chandrakirti compares this to a reflection of the moon in water that is stirred by a mild breeze:

> [*Homage to that compassion for*] migrators
> *Seen as evanescent and empty of inherent*
> *Existence like a moon in rippling water.*

Again, the example is to be imagined vividly in meditation; one has to visualize a reflection of the moon shimmering in constantly rippled water. Once a clear picture of this has formed, one considers oneself and other sentient beings in this way.

We see ourselves as quite substantial, solid and concrete; therefore, if, like the reflection of a moon in rippling water, we are changing every moment and yet conceive ourselves to be solid and steady, our self-conception is out of tune with the fact. From that viewpoint, we can develop a wish to leave cyclic existence, and when we extend this understanding to others, seeing that they too hold such a mistaken view, compassion is generated.

Just the fact that people are made, that their bodies and minds depend upon causes and conditions, is sufficient proof of impermanence. Once one understands that sentient beings are impermanent, it follows that there is no person separate from a collection of mind and body; this implies a realization that persons do not substantially exist as controllers of mind and body. Thus, 'compassion observing sentient beings who are only designated to phenomena' means that sentient beings are seen as qualified not only by the suffering of wandering in cyclic existence like a bucket in a well but also by impermanence – momentary disintegration – and lack of substantial existence. By reflecting on the fact that an unfounded conception of a solid, substantially existent self draws sentient beings into suffering, compassion is easily generated.

The third type of compassion is called 'compassion observing the unapprehendable'. Does this mean that one generates compassion for emptiness? But since emptiness is not a person, how could one? Tsong-ka-pa makes clear that it means 'compassion for sentient beings who are qualified by emptiness'.

Chandrakirti gives the example of the reflection of a moon in a calm lake. In this case, a meditator imagines a reflection of the full moon in a lake. The reflection is so brilliant and clear that if one did not know about the lake, one would think it was the moon; from every viewpoint it appears to be a moon. Then, one can mentally divide it into parts, like a pie, and ask oneself, 'Is this part a moon? Is that part? Is the collection of the parts a moon?' It appears to be a moon but is not.

Does this example mean that persons appear to be sentient beings but are not? Why have compassion if there are no sentient beings? However, this is not the meaning. Rather, sentient beings appear to exist *inherently* but do not. Just as when one examines the reflection of the moon in water, one cannot find a moon, so when the consciousness examining whether or not things exist in and of themselves analyses the bases of the designation 'person', it does not find anything that is a person. A person is only designated to mind and body, and yet this designatedly existent person is capable of performing functions.

Emptiness does not imply non-existence or non-functionality – unlike the moon in the water, which is not capable of performing the functions of a moon, or a snake imputed to a rope. If one considers each of the strands of a rope separately, each is not a snake. Together they are also not a snake, nor is the collection of them over time. Just so with sentient beings; neither the individual phenomena of mind and body nor their collection is the person; they are just the basis of the designation 'person'. No matter where one searches, one will not find anything that is a person. Still, a person is a dependent-arising, capable of performing functions, and not just a figment of imagination.

Chandrakirti gives the example of a water-moon so that an analogue of emptiness can be formulated and then used in developing a realization of emptiness itself, which is far deeper. The emptiness of the reflection of a moon in water is not just the fact that it is not a moon; rather, the example is a worldly analogue to the non-findability of phenomena under ultimate analysis. Just as the reflection of a moon in water appears to be a moon but is not, so sentient beings appear to be inherently existent, to be findable, to be concrete, existing in and of themselves, but are not. Also, a reflection's emptiness is its lack of inherent existence.

The Fifth Dalai Lama says in his *Sacred Word of Manjushri* that when one ascertains the sense of a concrete 'I', it will seem graspable and perceivable. It is said in the oral tradition that one will feel, 'If this does not exist, what could exist?' Thus, it seems that when one begins to feel that the doctrine of selflessness is wrong, one is just beginning the practice of Madhyamika. If the conception of inherent existence is so strong that it draws us into a condition of suffering in life after life, we will not be easily convinced that it is mistaken.

Through reasoned analysis, however, one can gain conviction that this conception has no foundation. Just as in dreams one is convinced that non-existent objects exist just because they appear very vividly, so it is with a falsely concrete 'I' which actually does not exist in that way at all. When one understands and becomes accustomed to the fact that this conception of objective existence is unfounded, one can generate a very strong wish to leave cyclic existence. Extending this understanding to others, one can easily generate a continual sense of compassion. In this way, the third compassion observes sentient beings who are qualified by non-inherent, non-true, non-analytically findable existence.

Just as by understanding emptiness one realizes that it is possible to eradicate cyclic existence and one thereby develops a firm decision to leave cyclic existence, so when one understands that others' suffering is also induced by the misconceptions of ignorance, one realizes that it is possible to eradicate all suffering and thereby develops a firm decision to free them from misery. Compassion is then a realistic expression of deep knowledge.

Tsong-ka-pa's

Illumination of the Thought
An Extensive Explanation of Chandrakirti's
'Supplement to the Middle Way'

Chapters one to five

The stanzas of Chandrakirti's root text are
numbered, indented, and italicized to
distinguish them from Tsong-ka-pa's
commentary.

Homage to Manjushri

INTRODUCTION

I bow down and go for refuge with great respect to the feet
of the revered guru Manjughosha and the father – the Superior
Nagarjuna – and his sons.

> May I always be protected by the King of Subduers,
> Sun of all teachers, treasure of all good explanations
> Of the profound and vast, unusual friend of all the world,
> Eye revealing the good path to migrators on the three levels.[1]

> May I always receive the blessed empowerment
> From guru Manjughosha, source of profundity
> In the retinue of countless Conquerors, unequalled
> In proclaiming the lion's roar of right discourse supreme.

> Homage from my heart to the prophesied Nagarjuna,
> Who explained as it is the middle way of dependent –
> Arising, free from extremes, the mind essence of the Sugatas[2]
> In the past, present, and future. Hold me then with the hook of
>   mercy.

> Homage to the feet of the glorious Aryadeva,
> Who ascended to high rank through that protector's precepts,
> Clarifying for migrators what he had realized,
> Attaining dominion of discourse teaching the good path.

I bow down with my head to the feet of Buddhapalita,
Who accomplished the word of the revered Manjughosha,
Illuminated the final thought of the Superior,[3]
And went to a place of Knowledge Bearer adepts.[4]

Homage to the honourable Chandrakirti and Shantideva,
Who completely and perfectly revealed the path
Of the great sage [Buddha], subtle and hard to realize,
The extraordinary essentials of Nagarjuna's system.

I have seen well with the eye of stainless intelligence
All the meanings of the uncommon essentials
In the tenets of Nagarjuna and Aryadeva
And commentaries of the three great charioteers.[5]

In order to remove the corruptions by the pollutions
Of interpretations by most who sought to teach this system
And because others have requested it I will explain at length
In full and correctly the *Supplement to the Middle Way*.

Here I will explain, in accordance with his own commentary,
Chandrakirti's *Supplement to the Middle Way (Madhyamakāvatāra)*, a great text settling without error the profound and the
vast. The explanation has four parts, the meaning of the title,
obeisance of the translators, the meaning of the text, and of the
conclusion.

MEANING OF THE TITLE

In Sanskrit, one of the four language families of India, the
title of this treatise is *Madhyamakāvatāra*. This is translated as
Supplement to the Middle Way. The 'Middle Way' here is
Nagarjuna's *Treatise on the Middle Way (Madhyamakashāstra)*
because Chandrakirti says, 'In order to supplement the *Treatise
on the Middle Way....*'[6] Furthermore, when in his own commentary Chandrakirti cites Nagarjuna's *Treatise* as a source,
he frequently says, 'From the *Middle Way....*' The *Middle
Way* should, therefore, be taken to mean Nagarjuna's *Treatise
on the Middle Way*, not other texts on the middle way[7] or any

of the other meanings of *madhyamaka* [such as a person holding the tenets of the middle way or the tenets themselves].

In his *Lamp for Wisdom (Prajñāpradīpa)* Bhavaviveka explains that based on the verbal root [*ka* meaning proclaim][8] of *madhyamaka*, the term *madhyamaka* indicates a treatise of tenets of the middle way. Therefore, even though only the word *madhyamaka* appears [in Chandrakirti's title], it should be understood as referring to the *Madhyamakashāstra*, Nagarjuna's *Treatise on the Middle Way*.

QUESTION: How does Chandrakirti's text supplement Nagarjuna's *Treatise on the Middle Way*?

ANSWER: One person [Jaya-ananda][9] says that in Nagarjuna's *Treatise* conventional and ultimate natures are not taught extensively, but that Chandrakirti teaches these two extensively here and in this way supplements Nagarjuna's *Treatise*.

This is not a good explanation because the forms of reasoning ascertaining suchness are far more extensive in Nagarjuna's *Treatise on the Middle Way* than in Chandrakirti's *Supplement*. Our own system on this is that Chandrakirti supplements Nagarjuna's *Treatise* in two ways, from the viewpoints of the profound and of the vast.

With respect to the first, Chandrakirti says that he composed the *Supplement* in order to indicate that the meaning of the middle way which he ascertained is not shared with other Madhyamikas [specifically, Svatantrikas]. He also says that he composed it in order to show that it is not suitable to explain the meaning of Nagarjuna's *Treatise* in accordance with the Mind-Only system (*Chittamātra* or *Vijñaptimātra*). Chandrakirti says in his own commentary, 'The learned should determine that this system is uncommon,'[10] and, 'This *Supplement* was written for the sake of unmistakenly indicating the suchness of the *Treatise* because, through not understanding suchness, this profound doctrine might be abandoned.'[11] Chandrakirti's *Clear Words (Prasannapadā)* says, 'The mode of dependent designation can be known from my *Supplement*.' Also, refutation of the Mind-Only system, which was not done at length in Nagarjuna's *Treatise* or in Chandrakirti's *Clear*

D

Words, is extensive here in the *Supplement*. Therefore, one way
in which this book supplements the *Treatise* is through its
good determination of the meaning of the *Treatise* from the
viewpoint of these two purposes [distinguishing the suchness
of the *Treatise* from the interpretations by Svatantrikas and by
Chittamatrins].

It also supplements the *Treatise* from the viewpoint of the
vast. According to the Superior Nagarjuna's system, the two
vehicles [Hinayana and Mahayana] are not distinguished by the
presence or absence of the wisdom realizing the very profound suchness [but by the vast methods]. Although Nagarjuna's *Treatise*, except for the topic of profundity, does not
indicate the features of vastness in the Mahayana, his text was
nevertheless composed in terms of the Mahayana rather than
the Hinayana.[12] This is so because extensive teaching of the
selflessness of phenomena through limitless forms of reasoning is
solely for Mahayana trainees and in Nagarjuna's *Treatise on the
Middle Way* such extensive teaching is given. Chandrakirti says
this very clearly in his own commentary to his *Supplement*,[13] 'It
is correct that the Mahayana was taught for the sake of clarify-
ing the selflessness of phenomena because [Buddha] wished to
give an extensive teaching [of the selflessness of phenomena]. In
the Hearer Vehicle the selflessness of phenomena is illustrated
only briefly.' I will explain this later (pages 174–6).

Thus, [Chandrakirti thought that] it would be very good to
fill in the gaps in the paths explained in the *Treatise on the
Middle Way* – supplying the other Mahayana paths of vastness
by way of the quintessential instructions of the Superior
Nagarjuna [as found in his *Precious Garland (Ratnāvalī)* and
Compendium of Sutra (Sūtrasamuchchaya)]. In order to fill these
gaps Chandrakirti set forth (1) the three practices done on the
level of a common being, (2) the ten grounds of a Learner
Superior, (3) the effect ground, and (4) the cultivation of
special insight through the steps of the fifth and sixth grounds.
The latter is an investigation by analytical wisdom of suchness –
the two selflessnesses – in dependence on calm abiding, the
entity of concentration.

When the meaning of Nagarjuna's *Treatise on the Middle Way* is considered, you should be mindful of these topics as set forth in Chandrakirti's *Supplement* and should keep in mind the stages of the path which are a composite of both the profound and the vast. If a person does not do this, he forsakes the two purposes of Chandrakirti's composing the *Supplement*.

Thus, the second way that this text supplements Nagarjuna's *Treatise on the Middle Way* is in supplementing the paths of the *Treatise* from the viewpoint of the vast.

OBEISANCE OF THE TRANSLATORS

Homage to the youthful Manjushri[14]

The meaning of the words is easy to understand.

Since this book presents ultimate knowledge *(paramārtha-abhidharma)*, the training in wisdom is central. Therefore, the translators paid homage to Manjushri in accordance with the former partitioning of Buddha's word [into three scriptural collections: knowledge *(abhidharma)*, sets of discourses *(sūtrānta)*, and discipline *(vinaya)*].[15]

1 *Homage to Compassion*

MEANING OF THE TEXT

This section has four parts, (1) expression of worship – a means of beginning to compose the text, (2) body of the text, (3) way that it was composed, and (4) dedication of the virtue of composing it.

EXPRESSION OF WORSHIP, A MEANS OF BEGINNING TO COMPOSE THE TEXT

This section has two parts, praise of great compassion without differentiating its types and homage to that compassion within differentiating its types.

PRAISE OF GREAT COMPASSION WITHOUT DIFFERENTIATING ITS TYPES

The honourable Chandrakirti, having assumed the task of making a supplement to Nagarjuna's *Treatise on the Middle Way*, does not state as his object of worship the Hearers and Solitary Realizers who are taken as objects of worship in other books. Furthermore, he indicates that, rather than praising Buddhas and Bodhisattvas, it is suitable to praise great compassion – the most excellent cause of Buddhahood, bearing the nature of thoroughly protecting all vulnerable sentient beings bound in the prison of cyclic existence; it is also the main cause called by the name of its effect, the blessed one *(bhagavatī)*. Chandrakirti says:

1   *Hearers and middling realizers of suchness*
    Are born from the Kings of Subduers.
    Buddhas are born from Bodhisattvas.
    The mind of compassion, non-dual understanding,
    And the altruistic mind of enlightenment
    Are the causes of Children of Conquerors.

2   *Mercy alone is seen as the seed*
    Of a Conqueror's rich harvest,
    As water for development, and as
    Ripening in a state of long enjoyment,
    Therefore at the start I praise compassion.

The discussion of this has two parts, compassion as the main cause and as the root of the other two causes of a Bodhisattva.

COMPASSION AS THE MAIN CAUSE OF A BODHISATTVA

This section has three parts, the way Hearers and Solitary Realizers are born from Kings of Subduers, the way Buddhas are born from Bodhisattvas, and the three main causes of Bodhisattvas.

The Way Hearers and Solitary Realizers are Born from Kings of Subduers

Hearers are so called because they listen to correct precepts from others and after attaining the fruit of their meditation – the enlightenment of a Hearer – they cause others to hear about that fact. They say, 'I have done what was to be done; I will not know another birth,' and so forth. Many such instances appear in the scriptures.

Although there are some Hearers – such as those in the formless realm – to whom this etymology does not apply, there is no fault because the features of an etymology do not have to apply to all instances for a term to be used as an actual name. For instance, the term 'lake-born' is used for a lotus grown from dry soil.

The Sanskrit word for Hearer, *Shrāvaka,* can also mean 'hearing and proclaiming' in the sense that they hear from Buddhas about the superior fruit or the path proceeding to Buddhahood and proclaim it to those of the Mahayana lineage seeking that path. The *White Lotus of Excellent Doctrine Sutra (Saddharmapuṇḍarīka)* says [in reference to Bodhisattvas who merely proclaim the path without practising it]:[16]

> O Protector, today we have become hearers.
> We proclaim the excellent enlightenment
> And set forth the terms of enlightenment.
> Thus we are like intractable Hearers.

For those two reasons these Bodhisattvas are similar to Hearers, but the actual meaning of hearing and proclaiming applies [only] to Hearers.

[Jaya-ananda] says that because the word 'excellent' is absent in the third line [of the quote from the *White Lotus*] the former enlightenment is the Mahayana and the latter the Hearer enlightenment. However, the thought of Chandrakirti's commentary is that the first is the Mahayana enlightenment and the second is the path proceeding to it.

OBJECTION: Bodhisattvas would [absurdly] have to be [Hinayana] Hearers because they hear the path of Buddhahood from Buddhas and proclaim it to trainees.

ANSWER: There is no such fault because the thought is that Hearers *merely* proclaim the Mahayana path; they themselves do not achieve even a similitude of it.

[In Chandrakirti's root text 'middling realizers of suchness' was translated into Tibetan as 'middling buddhas'.] In the commentary Chandrakirti[17] says that *tattva-buddha* applies to all three persons [Hearer, Solitary Realizer, and Buddha Superiors]. With regard to the meaning of this, some identify *tattva-buddha* as realization of suchness and apply it to all three. As will be explained, this is a good interpretation because it is said, '*Tattva* means suchness *(tathatā)*, and *buddha* means realization.'

When the term *buddha* is taken to mean 'realization of suchness', this applies to all three persons.

Though the term 'realizers of suchness' also indicates 'Solitary Realizers', it was translated [into Tibetan] as *buddha*. In general the term *buddha* should be rendered as 'Buddha' but here this is not appropriate. For it is also explained that *buddha* is used to indicate an *opening* of lotus petals and an *awakening* from sleep; therefore 'Buddha' is not the only translation.[18]

With respect to the meaning of 'middling', Solitary Realizers surpass Hearers through their superior feature of practising merit and wisdom for a hundred aeons. However, since they do not have the two collections of merit and wisdom, nor the compassion viewing all sentient beings at all times, nor omniscience and so forth, they are inferior to perfect Buddhas. Thus, they are middling.

One [Jaya-ananda][19] says that the meaning of Solitary Realizers' surpassing Hearers in terms of wisdom should be understood in accordance with Maitreya's statement in his *Ornament for the Realizations (Abhisamayālaṃkāra)*, 'They abandon the conception of objects [by realizing that object and subject are not different entities].' This is not correct because here in the Prasangika system it is said that both Hearers and Solitary Realizers realize that all phenomena do not inherently exist. [Jaya-ananda] himself asserts this [when later he says that Hearers and Solitary Realizers cognize the emptiness of all phenomena].[20]

In his commentary Chandrakirti[21] says that a Solitary Realizer's wisdom surpasses in its increase that of a Hearer. This 'increase' should be taken to mean proceeding higher and higher on the path. Solitary Realizers are intent on cultivating merit and wisdom over a hundred aeons; thus, unlike the Hearers, they are able to continue cultivating the path for a long time.

[Chandrakirti[22] says that Solitary Realizers do not collect merit and wisdom; however, they do have secondary or imputed collections.] The mere term 'collection' is indeed used for merit and wisdom in general, but it applies mainly to fully qualified merit and wisdom. As Haribhadra's *Clear Meaning Commentary (Abhisamayālaṃkāranāmaprajñāpāramitopadeshashāstravṛtti)* says, 'By being entities that thoroughly achieve it, they *hold* the great enlightenment; therefore, great compassion and so forth are collections.' Collections are said to hold their fruit through being the means of unmistakenly achieving highest enlightenment. Those that are not fully qualified are secondary. This is a contextual etymology of the original Sanskrit word for collection, *sambhāra*. [With letters added, *sam* comes to mean 'thorough achievement', *bhā* 'entity', and *ra* 'bearing'.][23]

Because Solitary Realizers' progress in merit and wisdom greatly exceeds that of Hearers, they are able to generate the wisdom of a Foe Destroyer *(Arhan)* during their final lifetime in the desire realm without depending on another master's teaching. Because they become enlightened – that is to say, attain or are in the process of attaining the state of a Foe Destroyer – for their own sakes alone, they are called 'Self-Enlightened' and also 'Self-Arisen'.

[With respect to the phrase 'Kings of Subduers'] the term 'Subduer' is indeed used for Hearer and Solitary Realizer Foe Destroyers, but since they are not *kings* of Subduers, only Buddhas are so called. This is because Buddhas have attained an excellent lordship of doctrine superior to Hearers, Solitary Realizers, or even Bodhisattvas and also because the word of Buddha rules these three in the sphere of doctrine. That Hearers and Solitary Realizers are born from Kings of Subduers means that they are issued forth by them.

QUESTION: How do Subduer Kings give birth to Hearers and Solitary Realizers?

ANSWER: When Buddhas come to the world, they teach dependent-arising without error. Those bearing the lineage of Hearers and Solitary Realizers listen to the modes of dependent-arising, think about what they have heard, and meditate on the meaning of what they have thought. Through these stages, the aims of Hearers and Solitary Realizers are fulfilled in accordance with the effect to which they aspire, and in this way Subduer Kings give birth to Hearers and Solitary Realizers.

OBJECTION: Although many of the Hearer lineage actualize enlightenment in the very life in which they hear the doctrine from a Buddha, those of the Solitary Realizer lineage do not do so. Therefore, it is incorrect that their aims are fulfilled through hearing, thinking, and meditating on meanings set forth by Subduer Kings.

ANSWER: There is no fault. Some bearing the lineage of Solitary Realizers become skilled in cognizing the ultimate just by listening to the Teacher's setting forth dependent-arising. However, they do not attain the nirvana of a Solitary Realizer in just that life during which they hear the doctrine. Still, a Solitary Realizer practitioner to whom a Buddha teaches dependent-arising will definitely achieve nirvana in another life. An example of this is a person's accumulating an action the effect of which must be experienced but not in the same life as when accumulated; however, the effect will definitely be experienced in another birth. Also, since Solitary Realizers hear, think, and meditate on just the doctrine formerly taught by a Buddha, the explanation that their aims are fulfilled is not intended to refer to this life only. Aryadeva's *Four Hundred* (*Chatuḥshataka*, VIII.22) says:

> Though one who knows suchness does not achieve
> Nirvana here, in another birth
> He will definitely attain it
> Without effort, as in the case of actions.

Nagarjuna's *Treatise on the Middle Way* (XVIII.12) says:

> Though the perfect Buddhas do not appear
> And Hearers have disappeared,
> A Solitary Realizer's wisdom
> Arises without support.

One [Jaya-ananda][24] asserts that this section in Chandrakirti's commentary[25] answers the doubt, 'It is seen that though dependent-arising is taught, some do not achieve the state of Hearers and so forth; thus, Hearers and so forth do not fulfil their aims through the teaching of dependent-arising.' Other [Tibetans][26] say that this answers the doubt that although it would be suitable for the effect to arise immediately after practising the meaning of dependent-arising and non-production, it does not, and, therefore, the effect might not arise later either.

These explanations are instances of not understanding the meaning of this section. Because there are greater doubts about the Subduer Kings' giving birth to Solitary Realizers, [doubts about this] should be singled out and eliminated [but according to these explanations Chandrakirti] did not do so.

The Way Buddhas are Born from Bodhisattvas

QUESTION: If Hearers and Solitary Realizers are born from Subduer Kings, from what are Subduer Kings born?

ANSWER: The perfect Buddhas are born from Bodhisattvas.

OBJECTION: Are Bodhisattvas not called 'Conqueror Children' because they are born from Buddhas' teaching? Since Bodhisattvas are Conqueror Children, how can Buddhas be born from Bodhisattvas? For example, the father of a child cannot be that child's child.

ANSWER: It is true that Bodhisattvas are the children of certain Conquerors; however, there are two reasons why Bodhisattvas cause Buddhas. Bodhisattvas are causes of Buddhas from the viewpoint of state because the state of a Tathagata Buddha is the fruit of that of a Bodhisattva. This indicates that Bodhisattvas cause Buddhas through being the substantial cause which is of the same continuum as that Buddha. The state of Buddhahood is only attained through one's formerly having developed the state of a Bodhisattva on the path of learning.

Bodhisattvas also cause Buddhas through causing them to bear the truth in the sense that, as it says in sutra, the venerable Manjushri as a Bodhisattva caused our own Teacher and other Buddhas to bear the altruistic mind of enlightenment at the very beginning. This establishes that Buddhas are born from Bodhisattvas from the viewpoint that a Bodhisattva, who is of a different continuum from the Buddhahood which another Bodhisattva will attain, acts as a cooperative cause of that Buddha.

OBJECTION:[27] [Chandrakirti states the position of] an objector who says that since Bodhisattvas are Conqueror Children, it is correct for them to be born from Conquerors, but the opposite is not feasible. [In answer] he says it is true that Bodhisattvas are Conqueror Children, thereby indicating that he accepts this.[28] Though it is necessary to give the reason why, despite this assertion, there is no contradiction in saying that Buddhas are born from Bodhisattvas, Chandrakirti – without giving any such reason – [goes on to] establish that Buddhas are born from Bodhisattvas. Thus [his procedure] is wrong because a doubt has already arisen with respect to the topic and has not been eliminated.

ANSWER: There is no such fault. With respect to the first reason why the root text says that Buddhas are born from Bodhisattvas, Chandrakirti explains the attainment of the fruit of Buddhahood through a Bodhisattva's practice on the path of learning. It is thereby known that a Bodhisattva is not the child of the Buddha that he himself becomes. Hence, when Chandrakirti says that it is true – meaning, 'Bodhisattvas are indeed born from Buddhas' – how could he be referring to a Bodhisattva's birth from the Buddha he becomes? Furthermore, one newly born as a Bodhisattva from the speech of our Teacher is a child of this Buddha, but this Buddha is not born from the Bodhisattva. Indeed, if one has intelligence, why would one not realize from the answer given in the commentary that the objector has not distinguished these two modes? Still, many senseless explanations have appeared with respect to this.

Buddhas praise Bodhisattvas because Bodhisattvas are the principal causes of Buddhas. There are four reasons for the praise. The first is that this excellent cause of Buddhahood is very profound and precious. The second is that through expressing worship to the cause – Bodhisattvas – praise of the fruit – Buddhas – is intended implicitly. The third reason is

that one should value and sustain the state of a novice Bodhisattva, for it is the shoot of the tree of Buddhahood that nourishes
all beings. Just as one who has seen the shoot, trunk, and so
forth of a medicinal tree bearing countless wished-for fruits
would cherish and sustain the leaves of the tree when they are
young and soft, so one should value and sustain the state of a
novice Bodhisattva with great effort. The fourth reason is that
when Bodhisattvas are praised in the presence of those who are
established in the three vehicles, such persons thereby definitely
enter into the Mahayana.

The *Pile of Jewels Sutra (Ratnakūṭa)* says, 'Kashyapa, it is like
this: For example, people bow down to a new moon and not
to the full moon. In the same way, Kashyapa, those who have
great faith in me should bow down not to Tathagatas but to
Bodhisattvas. Why? Tathagatas arise from Bodhisattvas. All
Hearers and Solitary Realizers arise from Tathagatas.' This
establishes through scripture that Buddhas are born from
Bodhisattvas. The two former reasons establish it through
reasoning.

Thus, here Chandrakirti does not directly honour Hearers,
Solitary Realizers, Buddhas, or Bodhisattvas – who are re-
nowned as objects of worship in other books. This is because
he honours the causes that are their roots.

The first two lines of the root text indicate that these four –
Hearers and Solitary Realizers, Buddhas, and Bodhisattvas –
are in an effect and cause relationship respectively. This is for
the sake of identifying the cause that is their ultimate root
[compassion].

Though Bodhisattvas are born from the teaching of Buddhas,
Chandrakirti does not need to explain this as he did for Hearers
and Solitary Realizers when he said that they are born from
Subduer Kings. He taught that Hearers and Solitary Realizers
are born from Subduer Kings in order to show that their root
ultimately derives from compassion. [In the following stanzas]
he indicates separately that the root of Bodhisattvas derives
from compassion.

2 *Causes of Bodhisattvas*

The Three Main Causes of Bodhisattvas

QUESTION: If Hearers and Solitary Realizers are born from Subduer Kings and if Subduer Kings are born from Bodhisattvas, what causes Bodhisattvas?

ANSWER: Chandrakirti's root text says:

ldef *The mind of compassion, non-dual understanding,*
And the altruistic mind of enlightenment
Are the causes of Children of Conquerors.

The main causes of Bodhisattvas are three, a compassionate mind which will be explained [in the following stanzas], a wisdom realizing the meaning of freedom from the two extremes with regard to things, non-things, and so forth, and an altruistic mind of enlightenment.

Chandrakirti says in his commentary that the altruistic mind of enlightenment is as shown in the quoted sutra.[29] The *Omnipresent Doctrine Sutra* says, 'One realizes the suchness of phenomena and generates the thought, "I will cause sentient beings to understand this nature of phenomena." This mind which is generated is called an altruistic mind of enlightenment.' This does not indicate all the characteristics of an altruistic mind generation because it takes cognizance of only one part – its objects of intent. The definition in Chandrakirti's commentary is also partial.[30] He says, 'One definitely generates an altruistic mind thinking, "I will relieve all these worldly beings from suffering and will definitely join them to Buddha-hood." ' The commentary does not mention taking cogni-zance of the object of attainment, one's own enlightenment.

However, Chandrakirti later shows in his commentary[31] that an altruistic mind of enlightenment is generated in de-pendence on compassion; he says, 'One wishes to attain Buddhahood, which is the cause giving rise to the marvellous taste of ambrosia of the excellent doctrine, which is charac-terized by the disappearance of all wrong thoughts, and which has the nature of being the friend of all beings.' Thus, he clearly mentions taking cognizance of the object of attainment, one's own enlightenment. Therefore, the complete definition of an altruistic mind generation is asserted to be the wish to attain highest enlightenment – the object of attainment – for the sake of all sentient beings – the objects of intent.

That such appears in [Jaya-ananda's] commentary is good. There is also no difference between what is said in Maitreya's *Ornament for the Realizations*[32] and this system.

Assigning these three practices as the causes of Bodhisattvas is the system of Nagarjuna's *Precious Garland* (174c–175):

> If you and the world wish to gain
> The highest enlightenment,
> Its roots are an altruistic aspiration
> To enlightenment firm like Meru, the king of mountains,
> Compassion reaching in all directions,
> And wisdom which relies not on duality.

This passage indicates that these three are the roots of enlighten-ment but does not explicitly show that these are the roots of a Bodhisattva; however, since root means 'beginning', Nagar-juna is indicating the three main causes of the beginning, and thus it can be known from the context that these are the main causes of Bodhisattvas.

Chandrakirti's teaching these three practices as the causes of Bodhisattvas occurs at the time of analysing the doubt,[33] 'If Hearers and Solitary Realizers are born from Buddhas, and Buddhas from Bodhisattvas, then from what are Bodhisattvas born?' Therefore, these three are not suitable to be causes for positing someone as a Bodhisattva; they are the causes producing a Bodhisattva.

OBJECTION: Is the lowest type of Bodhisattva, in relation to whom these three practices are assigned as causes, a novice Bodhisattva who has just entered the path or not? If he is, then it is incorrect to assign the altruistic mind generation of the Mahayana as a *cause* because as soon as he attains such a mind generation he is a Bodhisattva. Moreover, it is not feasible to assign the wisdom that does not rely on the two extremes as a cause of a Bodhisattva. This is because he initially generates a conventional mind of enlightenment and *then* trains in the Bodhisattva deeds – the six perfections – and thus only when training in the perfection of wisdom does he train in the wisdom not relying on the two extremes. On the other hand, if the lowest type of Bodhisattva in relation to whom these three are posited as causes is not taken as a novice Bodhisattva who has entered the path, then it would contradict the explanations of this lowest type of Bodhisattva as like a new moon and as like the shoot of a medicinal tree.[34]

ANSWER: The second position is not asserted because it would incur the fault as explained. Therefore, the first position is asserted, but it does not entail the faults stated above. The 'mind generation that precedes a Bodhisattva' refers to the time of cultivating mind generation and not to an actual mind generation that has been produced through having cultivated it. The difference between these two mind generations is like that between tasting the bark and the inside of sugar cane. Because the mere thought, 'I will attain Buddhahood for the sake of all sentient beings' is just verbal understanding, it is like tasting the bark of sugar cane, and although it is *called* an altruistic mind generation, it is not. Through having trained in this mind of enlightenment in accordance with quintessential instructions, special experience is generated that can redirect the mind well. This is like tasting sugar cane itself; therefore, it is fully qualified as a mind generation. Thinking of this,

Buddha said in the *Questions of Adhyashaya Sutra* (*Adhyāshaya-saṃchodana*):

> Verbalization is like the bark,
> Contemplating the meaning is like the taste.

A bearer of the Bodhisattva lineage with sharp faculties first seeks the view of suchness and then generates the altruistic mind. Therefore, as will be explained later (pages 123-4), the second fault is also not incurred.

'Non-dual understanding' does not refer to the absence of the dualistic appearance of object and subject [which occurs later on the path of seeing]. Chandrakirti's commentary[35] explains it as wisdom free from the two extremes; thus, it is not contradictory for it to occur prior to becoming a Bodhisattva. [Jaya-ananda's] explanation[39] that 'non-dual understanding' refers to an ultimate mind generation [which involves the non-appearance of subject and object and begins with the path of seeing] is quite senseless because 'non-dual understanding' must also indicate the wisdom that is a cause of a Bodhisattva newly entering the path.

COMPASSION AS THE ROOT OF THE OTHER TWO CAUSES OF A BODHISATTVA

Compassion is the root of the altruistic mind of enlightenment and non-dualistic wisdom; therefore, it is the chief of the three causes. Indicating this in his root text, Chandrakirti says:

> 2 *Mercy alone is seen as the seed*
> *Of a Conqueror's rich harvest,*
> *As water for development, and as*
> *Ripening in a state of long enjoyment,*
> *Therefore at the start I praise compassion.*

Mercy is important, like a seed, for the initial development of the marvellous harvest of a Conqueror. In the middle mercy is like water for increase higher and higher. At the end mercy is like the ripening of a fruit in a state of long enjoyment for trainees. Because mercy is asserted in this way, I, Chandrakirti, rather than praising Hearers, Solitary Realizers, Buddhas, Bodhisattvas, or the two other causes of Bodhisattvas, praise great compassion at the start of this treatise.

It is not that Chandrakirti *will* praise compassion; the immediately preceding indication of its importance in the beginning, middle, and end with respect to growing the harvest of a Conqueror is the praise. 'Mercy *alone*' indicates that unlike the three different examples of importance [seed, water, and ripeness] at the beginning, middle, and end for an external harvest, only compassion is important in the beginning, middle, and end for the harvest of a Conqueror.

The way that compassion's importance in the beginning is like a seed is this: Those who have great compassion generate a mind that observes their object of intent [the welfare of others] with the thought, 'In order to protect all suffering sentient beings pained by misery, I will relieve them from the suffering of cyclic existence and definitely establish them in Buddhahood.' Seeing that [the ability to do] this depends upon their own attainment of Buddhahood, they definitely generate a mind observing enlightenment with the thought, 'For their sake I will definitely attain highest enlightenment.' Because they understand that such a promise cannot be fulfilled if the practices of giving and so forth – illustrated [in Chandrakirti's commentary][37] by non-dualistic wisdom – are forsaken, they definitely engage in these practices, the chief of which is wisdom. Therefore, the seed of all Buddha qualities is great compassion. Referring to this Nagarjuna says in his *Precious Garland* (378):

> Who with intelligence would deride
> Deeds motivated by compassion
> And the stainless wisdom as is
> Taught in the Mahayana?

Nagarjuna says that all the meanings of the Mahayana are contained within the three: general practices induced by (1) the altruistic mind of enlightenment preceded by (2) compassion, and the particular practice of (3) wisdom free from the stains of conceiving the two extremes.

The importance of compassion in the middle is similar to water. For, although the seed of compassion initially grows into the shoot of an altruistic mind of enlightenment, if later it is not moistened again and again with the water of compassion, one will not amass the two extensive collections that serve as the causes of the fruit, Buddhahood. In that case one would actualize the nirvana of either a Hearer or Solitary Realizer. However, if the shoot of an altruistic mind of enlightenment is moistened again and again with the water of compassion, that will not happen; [one will actualize the enlightenment of a Buddha].

The importance of compassion at the end is similar to a state of ripeness. For, if one attains the state of a Conqueror but lacks the ripened state of compassion, one will not be a source of enjoyment and use by sentient beings as long as cyclic existence lasts. Also, the collection of Hearers, Solitary Realizers, and Bodhisattva Superiors [arising from] the transmission [of Buddha's word] from one to the other would not increase uninterruptedly. However, when great compassion operates continually at Buddhahood, the opposite occurs.

Through Chandrakirti's commentary on the meaning of these four lines you should gain firm conviction with respect to the teaching that it is necessary to train in these practices. You should think, 'If I wish to become a Mahayanist, my mind must first come under the influence of great compassion, and then in dependence on this I must generate from the depths of my heart a fully qualified altruistic mind of enlightenment. Once I have done this, I must engage in the general practices of Bodhisattvas and in particular must penetrate the profound view.'

3 Types of Compassion

HOMAGE TO GREAT COMPASSION WITHIN
DIFFERENTIATING ITS TYPES

This section has two parts, homage to compassion observing
sentient beings and homage to compassion observing phenomena and the unapprehendable.

Homage to Compassion Observing Sentient Beings

Chandrakirti says:

3 *Homage to that compassion for migrators who are*
Powerless like a bucket travelling in a well
Through initially adhering to a self, an 'I',
And then generating attachment for things, 'This is mine.'

The view of the transitory collection as a real 'I' generates the
view of that collection as real 'mine'. Therefore, these sentient
beings initially – prior to the view of the transitory adhering
to real 'mine' – adhere to an 'I' as a truth. The view of the
transitory apprehending a real 'I' thinks that the self – which
does not inherently exist – does so. Subsequently, the view of
the transitory apprehending real 'mine' generates attachment
for the truth of the 'mine', thinking, 'This is mine,' with
respect to phenomena other than the 'I', such as forms and
eyes.

Chandrakirti's homage to compassion observing sentient

beings is: Homage to compassion for migrators wandering powerlessly like a bucket travelling in a well.

QUESTION: In what way are migrators similar to a bucket in a well?

ANSWER: Sentient beings are the bearers of similarity, and a bucket in a well is the object of similarity, both having six features such as being tied.

The first feature is that these worldly beings are bound very tightly by the rope of contaminated actions and afflictions. In Chandrakirti's commentary,[38] the word 'these' should be applied to the other five features also.

The second is that the process [of cyclic existence] depends on being impelled by the mind, like the operator of the pulley mechanism. The third is that these sentient beings ceaselessly wander in the great well of cyclic existence from the Peak of Cyclic Existence down to the Most Tortuous Hell.

The fourth feature is that these sentient beings naturally and effortlessly go downward to bad migrations and must be drawn with great exertion upward to happy migrations. The fifth is that they have the three sets of thorough afflictions, the order of which cannot be determined one-pointedly. The three sets are (1) the afflictions of ignorance, attachment, and grasping, (2) the actions of compositional action and 'existence', and (3) the productions of consciousness, name and form, six sources, contact, feeling, birth, and ageing and death.[39]

The sixth feature is that every day these sentient beings are battered by the sufferings of pain and change, and the pervasive suffering of being so conditioned as to be always ready to undergo pain. Therefore, these sentient beings do not pass beyond the state of a bucket in a well.

Here the application of similarity by way of six features is not made merely for the sake of understanding the way that sentient beings wander in cyclic existence.

QUESTION: Then what is the purpose?

ANSWER: Previously Chandrakirti indicated that one who wishes to enter the Mahayana must initially generate great compassion, but he did not show how to generate compassion in meditation. Here, by showing the way that sentient beings wander powerlessly in cyclic existence he indicates how to generate great compassion through meditation.

By what agency do sentient beings enter into cyclic existence? By just this extremely unpeaceful, untamed mind. Where and how do they wander? From the Peak of Cyclic Existence to the Most Tortuous Hell without the slightest interruption in their circling. By what causes and conditions do they wander? By the power of contaminated actions and afflictions. They wander in bad migrations by the power of non-meritorious actions and afflictions, and in happy migrations by the power of meritorious and unmoving[40] actions and their afflictions. To be born in bad migrations the process operates automatically and without effort, but it is difficult to be born in happy migrations because great effort must be made to achieve their causes.

The *Topics of Discipline (Vinayavastu)* says that instances of leaving either a happy or a bad migration and going to a bad one are as numerous as the particles of this great earth and that instances of leaving a happy or a bad migration and going to a happy one are as few as the particles held on the tip of a fingernail.

Whenever any of the three groups of thorough afflictions in a round of dependent-arising is present, the two remaining groups are also operating in other rounds of dependent-arising. Therefore, the process is uninterrupted, and every day – like ripples in water – beings are tormented more than once by the three sufferings.

If your mind has not been affected by thinking about the way that you yourself wander in cyclic existence, then when you think about these modes of suffering in other sentient beings, there is no way that you as a beginner can find their suffering unbearable. Therefore, as Chandrakirti says in his commentary on Aryadeva's *Four Hundred*, first you should think about these in yourself and afterwards meditate on them in other sentient beings.

QUESTION: Can great compassion be induced merely by

meditating on the way that other sentient beings are tortured in cyclic existence by suffering and by the sources of suffering or is another aid needed?

ANSWER: In the world when suffering is seen in an enemy, not only is it not unbearable, but one delights in it. When a person who has neither helped nor harmed one is seen to suffer, one will in most cases pay no attention to that person. These [reactions] are due to not having a sense of pleasantness with respect to these persons.

When one sees a friend suffer, it is unbearable [in the sense that one must do something about it], and the degree of unbearability is just as great as one's sense of pleasantness toward him. Therefore, it is an important essential that one must generate a sense of strong cherishing and affection for sentient beings.

Among the kings of scholars, there are two systems concerning the means for generating a sense of pleasantness. Of the first, Chandrakirti says in his commentary to Aryadeva's *Four Hundred* that if sentient beings are considered to have been friends – such as parents – from beginningless time, then one can bear to plunge into cyclic existence for their sake. The great being Chandragomin and the king of scholars, Kamalashila, also presented it this way. The second is the system of the glorious Shantideva. These can be known from my explanations elsewhere [in the *Great Exposition of the Stages of the Path*].

Those who strive to train in great compassion through strongly cherishing sentient beings and reflecting on the ways in which those beings are tortured in cyclic existence make meaningful Chandrakirti's uncommon expression of worship. Those who otherwise claim to be skilled in this are like prattling parrots. This analogy applies to other situations as well.

Later (page 122) I will explain how this comes to be called compassion observing sentient beings.

Homage to Compassion Observing Phenomena and the Unapprehendable

In order to illuminate the compassions observing phenomena

and the unapprehendable from the viewpoints of the objects
observed, Chandrakirti says in his root text:

4abc   [*Homage to that compassion for*] *migrators*
          Seen as evanescent and empty of inherent
          Existence like a moon in rippling water.

Chandrakirti's homage to compassion observing phenomena is:
Homage to compassion viewing migrators as evanescent or
momentarily disintegrating, like a moon in water stirred by a
breeze. His homage to compassion observing the unapprehendable is: Homage to compassion viewing migrators as
empty of inherent existence though they appear to exist
inherently, like the reflection of the moon in water.

    In commenting on this, Chandrakirti says,[41] 'Homage to
that compassion' omitting 'for migrators', but his thought is
that the 'migrators' [of the previous stanza] are included as the
objects observed by the latter two compassions.

    An image of the moon appears in a portion of very clear
water that is covered by ripples from a mild breeze. The water
that serves as the basic object is [actually] apprehended prior
to the reflection, but the reflection is manifestly apprehended
as a real moon that disappears each day. The excellent ones,
namely, beings who are skilled in these ways, see momentary
impermanence and the emptiness of the nature of the moon as
it appears to be. As in the example, Bodhisattvas who have
come under the influence of compassion also see sentient beings
in an ocean – the view of the transitory – which is filled by a
vast blue river of ignorance. They see that this ocean in which
sentient beings abide is stirred by the winds of improper
thought and that the reflections of the beings' own wholesome
and unwholesome actions which are like the moon in the sky
are reflected in front of them. Bodhisattvas see sentient beings
with the suffering of composition – momentary disintegration – descending on them, and they see beings as empty of
inherent existence. Observing them, Bodhisattvas generate
great compassion, and, as explained earlier, their great
compassion arises from reflecting on the pleasantness of sentient

beings and on the ways in which they wander in cyclic existence.

Even though the view of the transitory is ignorance, Chandrakirti[42] explains ignorance separately [as a river flowing into the ocean of the view of the transitory] because he is referring to the ignorance that induces the view of the transitory – the conception of a self of phenomena.

At this point in his commentary[43] Chandrakirti says that the three compassions are distinguished by the objects that they observe, not by their subjective aspects. Therefore, all three types of compassion have as their subjective aspect the wish to free sentient beings from suffering; they are thereby similar in that they observe sentient beings. In discussing the first type of compassion Chandrakirti says (stanza 3a), 'Compassion for migrators', and in discussing the latter two types of compassion he says (4ab), 'Evanescent migrators.' In this way he shows that sentient beings are the objects observed.

Still, compassion observing phenomena does not observe just sentient beings, but those who momentarily disintegrate. Therefore, the objects of observation are sentient beings qualified by momentary impermanence. When one determines that beings disintegrate momentarily, the existence of a permanent, partless, and independent person is eliminated in one's mind. Thereby, one can ascertain the non-existence of sentient beings who are different entities from their mental and physical aggregates. At that time one understands that they are *designated* to the mere collection of the mental and physical aggregates. Sentient beings who are designated to the mere phenomena of the aggregates and so forth serve as the objects of observation, and thus this is called 'compassion observing phenomena'.

Impermanent sentient beings are just an illustration. Observing those who do not substantially exist in that they are not self-sufficient is also called 'observing phenomena'. Therefore, giving the name, 'observation of phenomena', to observation of sentient beings who are designated to mere phenomena is a contraction.

Compassion observing the unapprehendable also does not observe mere sentient beings. It observes a special object, sentient beings who are empty of inherent existence. 'Unapprehendable' means 'not truly existent' and refers to the referent object's not existing in the way that it is conceived to exist by a consciousness grasping at signs [of inherent existence]. Giving the name, 'observing the unapprehendable' or 'unapprehendable compassion' to the observation of sentient beings qualified by non-true existence is a contraction.

Many Tibetan commentators say that the second compassion observes momentary disintegration and the third non-inherent existence. These are explanations of those who have not understood well the subjective aspects and objects of observation of these two compassions. For, it is necessary to assert that both have the aspect of wishing to free sentient beings from suffering, and if momentariness and non-inherent existence were asserted as the objects of these aspects, then one compassion would have two discordant aspects as its mode of apprehension [because it would also have the aspect of realizing momentariness or non-inherent existence].

Sentient beings qualified by momentariness and non-inherent existence are put as the objects of observation of these two compassions. Thus, before a person can have these two in his mental continuum, he must ascertain that sentient beings are momentary and do not inherently exist. Then, in dependence on his previous ascertainment, the aspects of these two qualities must appear to his mind. However, it is not necessary that these compassions themselves apprehend sentient beings as impermanent or not inherently existent. [The appearance of these qualities to a compassionate mind due to previous ascertainment is sufficient.]⁴⁴

In both the basic text and the commentary Chandrakirti explains that the latter two compassions observe sentient beings qualified by the qualities explained above and says that mere sentient beings – who are not so qualified – are the objects of observation of the first compassion. Therefore, his giving the name, 'compassion observing sentient beings', to the first compassion is a convenient contraction.

It is wrong to assert that the first compassion must observe permanent, partless, and independent sentient beings. As for compassion in the continuums of those who have not found the view of selflessness, there are many instances of their generating compassion observing only sentient beings. There are also many instances of it observing sentient beings, not qualified by either of the two qualities explained above, in the continuums of those who have found the view of common personal selflessness or the view of suchness.[45] For instance, even though someone has completely refuted the referent object of a consciousness apprehending a pot to be permanent and has understood that the pot is impermanent, not every instance of his observing it is posited as an observation of a pot that is qualified by impermanence. Also, even though someone might not have understood that a pot is impermanent, not every instance of his observing it is put as an observation of a pot that is qualified by permanence.

No matter which of the three objects of observation these three compassions observe, each has the aspect of wishing to protect all sentient beings from all suffering. Therefore, they differ greatly from the compassion generated by Hearers and Solitary Realizers. When [practitioners] generate such compassions, they generate an altruistic mind of enlightenment, thinking, 'For the sake of sentient beings I will definitely attain the state of a Buddha.'

The compassion to which Chandrakirti offers worship is mainly initial compassion, but it is also the other compassions of Bodhisattvas. Thus, there is no contradiction in Chandrakirti's saying in his commentary at this point[46] that Bodhisattvas generate compassion.

QUESTION: Can all three types of compassion be a cause of Bodhisattvas when they first enter the path?

ANSWER: Those bearing the Mahayana lineage who are followers of fact [and not just words] initially seek knowledge of the true suchness [emptiness]. Once they have ascertained the ultimate well, they generate an altruistic mind of enlightenment, which is founded on generating great compassion for

sentient beings, and then train in the discipline of a Subduer –
the Bodhisattva deeds. Those bearing the Mahayana lineage
who are followers of faith cannot realize suchness first. They
generate an altruistic mind of enlightenment after which they
train in the Bodhisattva deeds such as searching for knowledge
of the meaning of reality. Shantirakshita's *Ornament of the
Middle Way (Madhyamakālaṃkāra)* says:

> First searching to know reality
> They ascertain well the ultimate
> And then generate compassion
> For the world obscured by bad views.
> Heroes effecting migrators' welfare,
> Skilled in the vast mind of enlightenment,
> They practise the Subduer's discipline
> Adorned with wisdom and compassion.
> Followers of pure faith generate
> The mind of perfect enlightenment,
> Assume the discipline of the Subduer,
> And strive for knowledge of reality.

Thus, there are two types of practitioners, and among them
there are cases of generating all three compassions prior to
becoming a Bodhisattva. [The followers of fact realize emptiness before becoming a Bodhisattva and thus can generate
compassion observing sentient beings qualified by non-
inherent existence.]

Even though one has previously found the view of suchness,
it is not contradictory that when training in the Bodhisattva
deeds [which include training in wisdom] one ascertains and
trains in the meaning of suchness. Not only is that not contradictory, it is the way it must be done.

Even though Chandrakirti, having offered worship, does
not explicitly promise to compose his text [as is customary],
there is no fault as Nagarjuna did the same in his *Treatise on the
Middle Way* and *Sixty Stanzas of Reasoning (Yuktiṣhaṣhṭikā)*.
Similarly, there are many instances of [an author's] making a
promise to write a book and not making an explicit expression
of worship as, for example, in Nagarjuna's *Friendly Letter*

(*Suhṛllekha*). Still, Chandrakirti implicitly promises to write the book when, wishing to begin it, he makes an expression of worship.

With respect to the factors causing others to become involved in the book, the *subject matter* is the profound and the vast. The *uncommon purpose* has been explained (pages 97–9). The *temporary essential purpose* begins with practising the meanings of the text that one has come to know [through hearing and thinking] and extends through progressing on the four paths [of a Bodhisattva – accumulation, preparation, seeing, and meditation]. The *final essential purpose* is [the attainment of] the effect ground – Buddhahood. The *relationship* of these is that the essential purposes depend on the purpose and that in turn depends on the text [the *Supplement*].

4   The Inexpressible Trail

ACTUAL BODY OF THE TEXT

This section has two parts, grounds of cause and effect.

CAUSAL GROUNDS

This section has three parts, ways of practising the paths of this system in general, those of practising on the level of common beings in particular, and presentation of the grounds of Bodhisattva Superiors.

WAYS OF PRACTISING THE PATHS OF
THIS SYSTEM IN GENERAL

QUESTION: If here in Chandrakirti's text the profound and vast paths of Bodhisattvas are arranged following the protector Nagarjuna, how are the stages of paths proceeding to Buddhahood asserted in the latter's system?

ANSWER: The purpose of settling the systems of the second Buddha – the honourable Nagarjuna – and so forth through hearing and thinking is to find great conviction in the ways to practise the pure path. You thereby will not be led astray by similitudes of paths. No matter how much you train in the texts of the Mahayana systems, hearing and thinking that do not develop any conviction in the ways to practise the path are cases of not properly accomplishing hearing and thinking.

Though you would have made effort in the Mahayana, you would have not extracted its essence well. You should strive to know the stages of progress on the path.

The honourable Nagarjuna made many explanations of portions of the path but wrote three books teaching the body of the path based on both the profound and the vast. As was quoted before, Nagarjuna's *Precious Garland* (174c–175) says:

> If you and the world wish to gain
> The highest enlightenment,
> Its roots are an altruistic aspiration
> To enlightenment firm like Meru, the king of mountains,
> Compassion reaching in all directions,
> And wisdom which relies not on duality.

And (378):

> Who with intelligence would deride
> Deeds motivated by compassion
> And the stainless wisdom as is
> Taught in the Mahayana?

Nagarjuna sets forth an identification of the six perfections, their benefit, and the training in them as well as in accompanying compassion (435–9):

> Briefly the virtues observed
> By Bodhisattvas are
> Giving, ethics, patience, effort,
> Concentration, wisdom, compassion, and so forth.

> Giving is to give away completely
> All one's wealth, ethics is to help others,
> Patience is to forsake anger,
> Effort, to delight in virtues;

> Concentration is unafflicted one-pointedness,
> Wisdom is to ascertain the meaning of the truths,
> Compassion is a mind that savors only
> Mercy and love for all sentient beings.

From giving there arises wealth, from ethics happiness,[47]
From patience a good appearance, from [effort in] virtue
Brilliance, from concentration peace, from wisdom
Liberation, from compassion all aims are achieved.

From the simultaneous perfection
Of all those seven is attained
The sphere of inconceivable wisdom,
The protectorship of the world.

Nagarjuna sets forth the basis of the deeds – a preliminary generation of the mind of enlightenment – and the progress on the ten Bodhisattva grounds through those deeds.

Nagarjuna's *Praise of the Element of Qualities (Dharmadhātu-stotra)* explains the generation of the altruistic mind of enlightenment – which is done after taking refuge – the enhancement of one's lineage through the ten perfections, and the ten Bodhisattva grounds. These rough condensations of the stages of the path are explained in detail in his *Compendium of Sutra*. There he sets forth the difficulties of attaining leisure, fortune, and faith in the teaching and the even greater difficulty of generating an altruistic mind of enlightenment. He presents the difficulty of attaining great compassion for sentient beings and the still greater one of gaining the means of abandoning the karmic obstructions [arising] from criticizing Bodhisattvas, thought to despise Bodhisattvas, demonic activities, forsaking the excellent doctrine, and so forth. Many such explanations are contained in his *Compendium of Sutra*.

Compared to the *Precious Garland* or the *Praise of the Element of Qualities,* the *Compendium of Sutra* is indeed clear. However, Shantideva – a great bearer of the master Nagarjuna's system – presents very clearly and extensively those stages of the path still more difficult to realize in general in both his *Compendium of Instructions (Shikshasamuāchchaya)* and *Engaging in the Bodhisattva Deeds (Bodhisattvacharyāvatāra).* He does this in particular in his *Compendium of Instructions* which is a commentary on the meaning of Nagarjuna's *Compendium of Sutra.* In explaining the *Compendium of Sutra* this book describes the initial thought on the importance of leisure and fortune and the extreme difficulty of finding both. It then sets forth helpful thought for extracting the essence of this life, generation of faith in general and of firm faith in particular through recalling the qualities of the Mahayana. It then explains generation of the aspirational mind of enlightenment, assuming vows of practice, giving away one's body, enjoyments, and roots of virtue, and the modes of maintenance, purification, and increase of these.

In his *Four Hundred* Aryadeva also presents the body of the profound and vast paths. Moreover, the body of the path is similar in Bhavaviveka's *Essence of the Middle Way (Madhyamakahṛdaya)*, Shantirakshita's *Ornament of the Middle Way*, and Kamalashila's three *Stages of Meditation on the Middle Way (Bhāvanākrama)*. Therefore, all the great bearers of the Superior Nagarjuna's system agree on the structure of the path.

The means for readily bestowing conviction in these paths and facilitating a beginner's entry to them can be known from the precepts found in the *Lamp for the Path to Enlightenment (Bodhipathapradīpa)* by Atisha, who was skilled in the two systems of the Mahayana [of Nagarjuna and Asanga].

WAYS OF PRACTISING ON THE LEVEL OF COMMON BEINGS IN PARTICULAR

QUESTION: This text presents both the vast and profound paths of Bodhisattvas as well as the fruit attained through them. Therefore, the stages of paths on the level of a common being – which are extremely important for a Bodhisattva – should have been taught here after the expression of worship but they were not. How could it be right for Chandrakirti to begin his explanation with the grounds of a Superior?

ANSWER: Since Chandrakirti explained those paths on the occasion of the expression of worship, he did not explain them after it. His purpose was to indicate that one who wishes to enter the Mahayana must first practise these paths by teaching the three main causes which, when cultivated in meditation, cause one to become a Bodhisattva.

Not only must you practise these first but you must also

E

do so once you have become a Bodhisattva. Since the wisdom
not relying on duality is the chief practice, you should understand, through its illustration, that you should train in the other
deeds such as giving. Nagarjuna's *Compendium of Sutra* says,
'A Bodhisattva should not apply himself to the profound
nature of phenomena bereft of skill in means. A union of
method and wisdom is the right application of a Bodhisattva.'
You must train in a union of the two collections and not place
confidence in being satisfied with a portion of method or
wisdom or in a mere one-pointedness of mind that lacks special
method and wisdom.

Some do not properly identify the measure of the object of
negation that is refuted by the reasoning analysing suchness and
consider that everything is refuted. They mistake all thought
as conceptions of true existence and consequently assert that
all presentations of conventionalities are based only on [the
ignorance of] others. They say that at the time of the fruit
[Buddhahood] there is nothing else except a Truth Body
which is mere suchness devoid of wisdom. They also assert that
Form Bodies are included within the mental continuums of
trainees. According to such people it would not be the system
of Chandrakirti's *Supplement* that Hearers and Solitary
Realizers are born from Kings of Subduers and Buddhas from
Bodhisattvas even though Chandrakirti proves these with scripture and reasoning. They would say that cultivation of the three
practices is posited only for others and is not the system of the
Bodhisattva Madhyamikas; thereby, they deprecate all paths
that must be practised from one's own point of view. For
them, the explanations that wandering sentient beings who are
empty of inherent existence are like a bucket in a well in six
ways would only be self-contradictory. Thus, you should know
that, beginning with the expression of worship, they have explained the meaning of the text incorrectly.

The ways of training in giving and so forth are also explained
in connection with the grounds of Superiors, but you should
understand and strive now to practise the many deeds that are
essential even from the level of a common being.

PRESENTATION OF THE GROUNDS OF BODHISATTVA
SUPERIORS

This section has three parts, presentation of the ten grounds in common, of the individual ones, and their features.

PRESENTATION OF THE TEN GROUNDS
IN COMMON

Chandrakirti's explanation here of eleven grounds – the Very Joyful and so forth – is based on Nagarjuna's rough presentation of the ten grounds and the eleventh [Buddhahood]. Nagarjuna's *Precious Garland* (440) says:

> Just as the eight levels of Hearers[48]
> Are explained in their vehicle,
> So are the ten Bodhisattva
> Grounds in the Mahayana.

Chandrakirti also bases his explanation on the *Sutra on the Ten Grounds (Dashabhūmika)*.

When Chandrakirti[49] describes the ten grounds – the Very Joyful and so forth – as ten mind generations, he is referring to ultimate mind generations [and not conventional ones]. With respect to the nature of the ten grounds which are assigned to ultimate mind generations, Chandrakirti's commentary[50] says, 'When a Bodhisattva's uncontaminated wisdom, conjoined with compassion and so forth, is divided into parts, each part is called a "ground" because it is a base of qualities.' The four topics by which the grounds are explained are (1) their nature, (2) the qualities with which they are thoroughly conjoined, (3) the way they are called 'grounds', and (4) by etymology.

In accordance with Vasubandhu's *Treasury of Knowledge (Abhidharmakosha)*, some persons [Jaya-ananda and some Tibetans][51] explain the nature of 'uncontaminated wisdom' as uncontaminated in the sense of not being amenable to the increase of contaminations. They have not understood the uncommon meaning of 'uncontaminated' in this system. In our own system the contaminated is anything polluted by either ignorance – the conception of true existence – or its predisposing latencies. The uncontaminated is wisdom free from those pollutions; as Chandrakirti's *Clear Words*[52] says, '. . . not from the viewpoint of the nature of objects of the uncontaminated wisdom in those *free from the obscurations of ignorance.*'

Before achieving Buddhahood, a mind that is not polluted by predisposing latencies of ignorance is none other than the nonconceptual wisdom of the meditative equipoise of Superiors. It is 'alternating' in the sense that when Superiors rise from meditative equipoise, they become polluted by pre-disposing latencies.

Up to and on the seventh ground pollution can occur through ignorance. However, for Bodhisattvas on the eighth ground as well as for Hearer and Solitary Realizer Foe Destroyers, polluting ignorance has been extinguished; therefore, pollution occurs for them not by way of ignorance but through predisposing latencies of ignorance.

In his commentary[53] Chandrakirti says that the first ground 'is called non-dualistic wisdom'. This refers to the lack of a dualistic appearance of object and subject as if distant and cut off from each other. It does not refer to a wisdom that has merely abandoned the two extremes [as does the non-dual understanding among the three practices of common beings].

The books of the master Chandrakirti contain many references to 'knowledge' and 'wisdom' free from the darkness of ignorance. Therefore, it would be an extremely deprecating denial to link ignorance and the predisposing latencies of ignorance with all knowledge and propound that according to this master's system wisdom disappears when ignorance and its predispositions are extinguished. These explanations are on a par with the Forder (*Tirthika*) Mimamsakas' assertion that if the pollutions were extinguished, so would be the mind. Saying that there is no wisdom in a Superior's meditative equipoise is also similar. Nagarjuna's *Precious Garland* (363d–364ab) says:

Those who see thus are liberated.
What sees [suchness]? By convention
It is said to be the mind.

By what functioning of a subject is suchness directly seen? In answer to this question, Nagarjuna says that conventionally the mind sees suchness directly. Also, his *Praise of the Element of Qualities* says:

When a metal garment which has become stained with
Contaminations and is to be cleansed by fire
Is put in fire, its stains
Are burned but it is not.

So, with regard to the mind of clear light
Which has the stains of desire and so forth
Its stains are burned by wisdom's fire
But not clear light, its suchness.

When a dirty garment, woven from threads of stone, is put in a fire, its stains are burned away but not the garment. Similarly, when the stains of the mind are burned by the fire of wisdom, the stains are burned, but the mind of clear light does not become non-existent.

A Bodhisattva Superior's wisdom of meditative equipoise and that belonging to Hearer and Solitary Realizer Superiors are similar since they directly cognize the nature of phenomena and are devoid of pollution by the predisposing latencies of ignorance. However, the differences that cause one, and not the other, to be described as a Bodhisattva Superior ground are that the one is influenced by great compassion and possesses the powers of the twelve hundred features and so forth whereas the other does not. Also, as explained earlier, there is a great difference as to whether or not direct cognition of suchness occurs from extending one's mind to the profound meaning [of emptiness] during the paths of accumulation and preparation through the use of limitless forms of reasoning pertaining to the meaning of suchness – the two selflessnesses.

Chandrakirti's statement,[54] 'When divided into parts,' refers to the individual grounds that are the earlier and later parts of the one uncontaminated wisdom – the whole – divided into individual stages. A 'ground' (*bhūmi*, literally 'earth') is like the earth because it acts as a source or base of auspicious qualities.

These points indicate that all ten ultimate grounds are assigned as only non-conceptual wisdoms. Though they are similar, individual grounds such as the Very Joyful are posited, and this is done from four points of view. The first feature is that the first ground has twelve sets of a hundred qualities, the second ground has twelve sets of a thousand qualities, and so forth, and – as will be explained later – the number of qualities increases progressively.

[The twelve sets of a hundred qualities during one instant on the first ground after a Bodhisattva has risen from meditative equipoise are:

1 seeing a hundred Buddhas in one instant
2 receiving the blessings of a hundred Buddhas
3 going to a hundred Buddha Lands
4 illuminating a hundred lands
5 vibrating a hundred worldly realms
6 living for a hundred aeons
7 seeing with true wisdom the past and future of a hundred aeons
8 entering into and rising from a hundred meditative stabilizations
9 opening a hundred different doors of doctrine
10 ripening a hundred sentient beings
11 emanating a hundred versions of one's own body
12 surrounding each of the hundred bodies with a hundred Bodhisattvas

The number increases with each ground:

first: one hundred
second: one thousand
third: one hundred thousand
fourth: one hundred ten million
fifth: one thousand ten million
sixth: one hundred thousand ten million
seventh: one hundred thousand ten trillion
eighth: a number equal to the particles of a billion worlds

ninth: a number equal to the particles of ten million billion worlds
tenth: a number equal to the particles of an inexpressible
   number of an inexpressible number of Buddha Lands.[55]

The second feature is the attainment of greater and greater
majesty of power. Though this is explained [by Jaya-ananda][56]
as vibrating a hundred lands, a thousand lands, and so forth,
such is included in the increase of the number of qualities
[which is the first feature]. Therefore, this feature should be
taken as the increase higher and higher of the power for
purifying the stains of the individual grounds and the power
for advancing on the paths of these grounds.

The third feature is a surpassing perfection – of giving on the
first ground, ethics on the second ground, and so on [patience
on the third, effort on the fourth, concentration on the fifth,
wisdom on the sixth, skill in means on the seventh, aspirational
prayer on the eighth, power on the ninth, and supreme wisdom
on the tenth].

The fourth feature is the higher and higher increase of births
of fruition – on the first ground birth as a king ruling Jam-
budvipa [this world], on the second as a king ruling the four
continents, and so forth [as a king ruling the Land of the
Thirty-Three on the third ground, the Land Without Combat
on the fourth, the Joyous Land on the fifth, the Land of Liking
Emanation on the sixth, of Controlling Others' Emanations
on the seventh, as a great Brahma lord of a thousand worlds
on the eighth, as a great Brahma lord of a million worlds on
the ninth, and as the Devaputra Maheshvara of the Highest
Land on the tenth].[57]

Since the non-conceptual wisdoms of the individual grounds
vary greatly in terms of inferior and superior abilities – such as
the number of qualities that are present – individual grounds
are posited. The grounds should not be understood as just
meditative equipoise because the features subsequent to
meditative equipoise that exist on each ground are included in
that particular ground. The mode of division into individual
grounds should be understood as explained; it is impossible

to divide these ultimate grounds by making a differentiation in terms of their object of observation or aspect. The *Sutra on the Ten Grounds* says:

> Just as the wise cannot express or see
> The trail of any bird across the sky,
> So none of the grounds of Conqueror Children
> Can be expressed. Then how can one listen?

Though a bird crosses the sky, the wise of the world cannot describe its trail in words, or see it in their minds. In the same way, though the ultimate grounds – like birds – progress through the sky of the nature of phenomena, even interpreters who are Superiors cannot describe the mode of progress in the way that Superiors themselves experience it. Thus, listeners cannot hear about the grounds the way they are perceived.

5 Very Joyful

PRESENTATION OF THE INDIVIDUAL GROUNDS

This section has three parts, the five grounds, the Very Joyful and so forth; the sixth ground, the Manifest; and the four grounds, the Gone Afar and so forth.

THE FIVE GROUNDS, THE VERY JOYFUL AND SO FORTH

This section has five parts, the first ground, the Very Joyful; the second, the Stainless; the third, the Luminous; the fourth the Radiant; and the fifth, the Difficult to Overcome.

FIRST GROUND, THE VERY JOYFUL

This section has three parts, entity of the ground being qualified described in brief, features qualifying the ground in detail, and the conclusion by way of expressing the features of the ground.

ENTITY OF THE GROUND BEING QUALIFIED DESCRIBED IN BRIEF

Chandrakirti's root text says:

4c–5b   *The mind of a Child of a Conqueror overpowered*
With compassion to liberate migrators,
Dedicated with Samantabhadra's aspirations,
And abiding in joy is called the first.

When a Conqueror Child abides on the first ground, his mind apprehends non-inherent existence, in the manner explained above, as a special feature of migrators who are the objects observed by his compassion. His mind has been influenced by great compassion for the purpose of liberating migrators, and his virtues are thoroughly dedicated with the aspirational prayers of the Bodhisattva Samantabhadra. This ultimate mind of a Bodhisattva – abiding in the non-dualistic wisdom called the 'Very Joyful' and illustrated by the number of qualities and so forth that are its effects – is called the first supramundane mind.

The ten innumerable hundred thousands of prayer petitions planted by a first grounder – such as the ten great petitions in the *Sutra on the Ten Grounds* – are included in Samantabhadra's aspirational prayers, to which Chandrakirti refers in his root text in order to include all such prayers. These are the *Aspirational Prayers for Auspicious Deeds (Bhadrachāryapranidhāna)*, and among them two stanzas are said by Shantideva in his *Compendium of Instructions* to be unsurpassed dedications:

> I dedicate all these virtues
> To my training in accordance
> With the knowledge of the hero Manjushri
> And likewise of Samantabhadra as well.

> With the dedications so highly praised
> By all the Conquerors of the three times
> To auspicious deeds I dedicate
> In all ways these roots of virtue.

Chandrakirti's commentary[58] says that just as Hearers on the path of preparation are not said to be approaching the first fruit [of a Stream Enterer], so the great of the great Bodhisattvas practising with belief who are just about to become first grounders, are on a level where the mind of enlightenment has not yet been generated. Chandrakirti is referring to the non-generation of an ultimate mind of enlightenment. It has already been explained that in general the aspiration to highest enlightenment has been generated even before this time and that such persons are also accepted by this system as Bodhisattvas. In his *Compendium of Instructions* Shantideva also establishes through many sutras that ordinary beings can generate a mind of enlightenment. Therefore, the assertion that [those on the paths of accumulation and preparation] are 'imputed Bodhisattvas' is wrong.

OBJECTION: In his *Compendium of Knowledge (Abhidharmasamuchchaya)* Asanga explains that when one becomes a Hearer on the path of preparation [who will attain the fruit of Stream Enterer] in a single session and until one attains the first fruit, one is an approacher to the fruit of Stream Enterer. Therefore, Chandrakirti's example is not established.

ANSWER: Vasubandhu's *Treasury of Knowledge* explains that those approaching the fruit of Stream Enterer have attained a Superior path; however, Asanga's *Compendium of Knowledge* does agree with the objector. These two discordant systems arose, and the master Chandrakirti is in agreement with the *Treasury of Knowledge*. This accords with Nagarjuna's *Compendium of Sutra* where it is said[59] that giving one meal for one day to a follower of doctrine [a person on the path of preparation] generates immeasurably greater merit than giving a hundred divine tastes of food and divine clothing each day for as many aeons as there are sands in the banks of the Ganges to as many followers of faith [persons on the path of accumulation] as there are particles in all the realms of the world. Further, giving one meal for one day to a person on the eighth level [an approacher to the fruit of Stream Enterer] generates immeasurably greater merit than giving as before to as many followers of doctrine as described above.

A follower of faith is clearly on the path of accumulation, and a follower of doctrine is clearly on that of preparation [therefore, a person on the eighth level is on the path of seeing, a Superior path].

FEATURES QUALIFYING THE FIRST GROUND IN DETAIL

This section has three parts, features beautifying one's own

continuum, those outshining others' continuums, and the surpassing feature on the first ground.

Features Beautifying One's Own Continuum
This section has two parts, individual features and features in
brief.

*Individual Features Beautifying One's Own Continuum on the
First Ground*
This section has three parts, the feature of attaining a meaningful name, four features of birth in the lineage and so forth, and
three of advancing to higher grounds and so forth.

Feature of Attaining a Meaningful Name on the First Ground
Chandrakirti's root text says:

5cd   *Then, having thus attained that mind*
        He is called a 'Bodhisattva'.

From the time of entering the first ground, the Bodhisattva –
because of having attained that ultimate mind – is called an
'ultimate Bodhisattva'. Once having passed beyond the level
of an ordinary being he is not called by any other name discordant with this term because he has become a Bodhisattva
Superior. The *Cloud of Jewels Sutra (Ratnamegha),* which
Chandrakirti quotes in his commentary,[60] says, 'One having
the great supreme qualities, [the fourth and last level] of the
path of preparation, has not attained the ground of an ultimate
Bodhisattva.' Thereby, it is known that [on the first ground]
one is called a 'Bodhisattva' with the qualification 'ultimate'.
  The *Two Thousand Five Hundred Stanza Perfection of Wisdom
Sutra (Sārdhadviśāhasrikāprajñāpāramitā)* says, 'In what way
does he know [all phenomena]? As non-arisen, non-produced,
and false, not in accordance with the imputations by or findings
of childish common beings. Therefore, he is called a Bodhisattva.' This implicitly indicates that one who understands
the suchness of phenomena in the way that a Superior does is
called a Bodhisattva. This also refers to an ultimate Bodhisattva

and does not indicate that among common beings there are no qualified Bodhisattvas.

Four Features of Birth in the Lineage and So Forth on the First Ground

Chandrakirti's root text says:

6 *Born in the Tathagata lineage*
  He completely forsakes the three links.
  The Bodhisattva attains an excellent joy
  And can vibrate a hundred world-systems.

He is born into the lineage of the Tathagatas because, abiding on the first ground, he has passed beyond all levels of ordinary beings, Hearers, and Solitary Realizers and has generated in his continuum the paths certain to proceed to Buddhahood. He will not go to other paths and is of definite lineage with respect to his own path. This first ground Bodhisattva directly sees personal selflessness – that a person does not exist of his own nature. Thereby, he abandons all three links – the [artificial] view of the transitory, the [afflicted] doubt which is a subtle increaser [of contamination],[61] and holding [bad] ethics and codes of behavior as superior. He abandons them in the sense that they will not arise again – meaning that the seeds of these three are abandoned.

The path of seeing abandons the artificial but not the innate form of the view of the transitory collection as a real 'I' and 'mine'.

QUESTION: Why does Chandrakirti mention only these three? Other afflictions to be abandoned by the path of seeing are also abandoned.

ANSWER: There are two ways of interpreting the thought of sutras setting forth this topic, but the superior one accords with the explanation given in Vasubandhu's *Treasury of Knowledge*:

Not wishing to go, mistaking
The path, and doubting the path
Obstruct progress to liberation.
Therefore the three are indicated.

For example, three main obstacles confront one who intends to go to another area – not wishing to go, mistaking the path, and having doubts about it. Similarly, there are three main obstacles to progressing toward liberation. The first [the view of the transitory collection as real 'I' and 'mine'] causes fear with respect to liberation as a result of which one does not wish to proceed there. The second [holding bad ethics and codes of behavior as superior] is a case of mistaking the path through relying on another one. The third [doubt] causes hesitation with respect to the path. Therefore, Chandrakirti mentions these three.

A first ground Bodhisattva has, as was explained before, entered a definite lineage. He has attained the qualities of its fruits and is free from the faults abandoned by this ground. Therefore, extraordinary joys are generated. On account of his many great joys, the Conqueror Child maintains an excellent joy, and because of his superior joys this ground is called the Very Joyful.

He also becomes able to vibrate a hundred different world systems.

Three Features of Advancing to Higher Grounds and so forth

Chandrakirti's root text says:

7abc   *Advancing from ground to ground he ascends,*
        Now all his paths to bad migrations have ceased,
        All the levels of ordinary beings are ended.

He is very enthusiastic to advance from the first to the second ground, and he will ascend to higher grounds. As soon as he attains the first ground, all paths going to a bad migration cease for the Bodhisattva.

OBJECTION: Once one attains forbearance [which is the third of four levels] on the path of preparation, is it not impossible to go to a bad migration by the power of former actions (*karma*)? What need is there to say that paths to bad migrations cease for one who has attained the first ground?

ANSWER: The impossibility of going to a bad migration once one attains forbearance on the path of preparation is not a case of having overcome the seeds leading to a bad migration through their antidotes but through an incompleteness of their causes. Here on the first ground, the seeds are overcome by means of their antidotes. Furthermore, Asanga's *Compendium of Knowledge* explains that the mental and physical aggregates (*skandha*), constituents (*dhātu*), and so forth of bad migrations are abandoned by the path of seeing.

When a Bodhisattva attains the first ground, all levels of a common being end for him.

Features Beautifying One's Own Continuum in Brief
Chandrakirti's root text says:

7d   *He is shown to be like the eighth Superior.*

When the four abiders in and four approachers to the fruit are counted downwards from Foe Destroyer,[62] the eighth Superior is an approacher to the fruit of Stream Enterer. The features of abandonment and realization concordant with this approacher's level arise by virtue of his having attained the Superior doctrine [or path]. A Bodhisattva's extinguishing of faults and arising of auspicious qualities – which are due to his having attained the first ground – are shown in a similar manner to those of an eighth Superior.

Features Outshining Others' Continuums
This section has three parts, on the first ground outshining Hearers and Solitary Realizers by way of lineage, on the seventh ground outshining Hearers and Solitary Realizers by way of intelligence, and the meaning established by these teachings.

On the First Ground Outshining Hearers and Solitary Realizers by way of Lineage
Chandrakirti's root text says:

8abc   *Even those abiding in the first mind of complete enlightenment*
       Overcome those born from the speech of the Subduer Kings
       And Solitary Realizers through their own merit's increase.

Not only those abiding in the second mind of complete enlightenment and so forth but even those in the first mind of enlightenment, the Very Joyful, overcome or outshine Hearers – who are born from the speech of Subduer Kings – and Solitary Realizers through the force of the merit of their conventional mind of enlightenment and compassion. Their merit exceeds that of the Hearers and Solitary Realizers. This feature is different from those explained earlier.

The *Liberation of Maitreya Sutra* (*Maitreyavimokṣha*) says, 'O child of good lineage, it is like this: For instance, because of the great nature of his lineage a prince with the royal name outshines all the principal elder ministers soon after his birth. In the same way, a novice Bodhisattva generates an [ultimate] mind of enlightenment and is born in the lineage of a Tathagata King of Doctrine. Soon thereafter, through the force of his altruistic mind of enlightenment and compassion he outshines Hearers and Solitary Realizers, who have maintained pure behaviour for a long time. Child of good lineage, it is like this: For example, soon after its birth, the offspring of a great king of eagles[63] has power in his wing and clarity of eye that none of the older birds have. Similarly, a Bodhisattva who has generated the first [ultimate] mind of enlightenment has taken birth in the lineage of a great Tathagata king of eagles. As an offspring of the king of eagles he overpowers others through the strength of his wings to generate an aspiration to omniscience, and he has the pure eye of a special thought. These features do not occur in any of the Hearers and Solitary Realizers who have practised renunciation for a hundred thousand aeons.'

In his commentary [Jaya-ananda][64] explains these two passages [in the *Liberation of Maitreya Sutra*] as referring to conceptual mind generation. However, the references to a 'novice Bodhisattva' and 'soon after generating a mind of enlightenment' are made in terms of an ultimate mind generation. Previously (versa 6a) Chandrakirti explained that birth in the Tathagata lineage takes place on the first ground [using the example of an eighth Superior (7d)], but aside from the use of different examples [those of a prince and an eagle's offspring and of an eighth Superior], both passages [the explanations of birth in the Tathagata lineage in the root text and in the *Liberation of Maitreya Sutra*] mean the same.[65] Furthermore, the meaning of these three lines in the root text appears to be an abridgement of that in the sutra. Many texts such as Maitreya's *Ornament for the Mahayana Sutras (Mahāyānasūtrālaṃkāra)* explain that mind generation of special pure thought [mentioned above in the *Liberation of Maitreya Sutra* as 'special thought'] refers to generating a mind of the first ground.

OBJECTION: Then, you do not assert that Hearers and Solitary Realizers are outshone when a Bodhisattva who is a common being generates the conventional mind of enlightenment?

ANSWER: It is not so; we do assert such. The *Liberation of Maitreya Sutra* says, 'O child of good lineage, it is like this: Even though a diamond has been broken, it outshines all excellent golden ornaments; it does not lose the name "diamond", and it banishes all poverty. In the same way, O child of good lineage, even though the diamond-like generation of an aspiration to omniscience lacks urgency, it overpowers all golden adornments of the qualities of Hearers and Solitary Realizers. [With this aspiration] one will not lose the name 'Bodhisattva', and all poverty of cyclic existence is overcome.' Shantideva quotes this sutra in his *Compendium of Instructions* as a source for the unsuitability of looking down on a Bodhisattva who lacks the Bodhisattva deeds, and it never happens that one who has attained a ground has a mind of enlightenment bereft of the Bodhisattva deeds. [Therefore, this sutra refers not to an ultimate but to a conventional mind generation.]

On the Seventh Ground Outshining Hearers and
Solitary Realizers by way of Intelligence

Chandrakirti's root text says:

8d *On the Gone Afar he surpasses them with his intelligence.*

When a Bodhisattva arrives at the seventh ground, the Gone Afar, he outshines Hearers and Solitary Realizers not only by way of his conventional mind of enlightenment but also through the power of his intelligence – his ultimate mind generation.

The *Sutra on the Ten Grounds* says, 'O Conqueror Children, it is like this: For example, merely through being born in a royal lineage, a prince having the royal name outshines all the groups of ministers because of the king's magnificence but not by the force of his own mind. When he matures, his power of intelligence is generated, and he greatly surpasses all the ministers' activities. In the same way, O Conqueror Children, as soon as they generate an [ultimate] mind of enlightenment, Bodhisattvas outshine all Hearers and Solitary Realizers by the greatness of their special thought but not by the power of their intelligence. However, a Bodhisattva on the seventh ground greatly surpasses all the activities of Hearers and Solitary Realizers through abiding in the greatness that is knowledge of his own sphere.'

'As soon as they generate an [ultimate] mind of enlightenment' refers to the time of [attaining] the first ground. Thus, it is an [ultimate] mind generation of special pure thought.

A Bodhisattva outshines Hearers and Solitary Realizers through the generation of his power of intelligence only on the seventh ground, the Gone Afar, and above. On the sixth ground and below he does not outshine them through his power of intelligence.

Chandrakirti's condensed commentary[66] on this shows that 'surpassing all the activities of Hearers and Solitary Realizers' means surpassing them through intelligence. [The sutra] explains 'the power of intelligence' as 'abiding in the greatness that is knowledge of his own sphere'. This is the greatness of knowing cessation, the limit of reality, the sphere of a Bodhisattva.

With regard to the meaning of this:

1 Some say that although there is no difference between the wisdom entities of the seventh and the sixth grounds and below, the wisdoms of the earlier grounds are incapable of abandoning obstructions to omniscience, whereas the wisdom of the seventh

ground has this capacity. Thus, the latter can outshine Hearers and Solitary Realizers from the viewpoint of intelligence and the former cannot.

2 Others explain that on the seventh ground and above a Bodhisattva is capable of leaping over [certain levels of] meditative stabilization.

3 Others say that a seventh ground Bodhisattva outshines Hearers and Solitary Realizers through intelligence because the wisdom of the seventh ground approaches the irreversible eighth ground.

The first of these three interpretations is not correct. The [Prasangika] system asserts that all conceptions that persons truly exist are instances of afflicted ignorance, and to abandon these conceptions in such a way that they will not be produced again, it is necessary to extinguish their seeds. Since this abandonment is common to Hearer and Solitary Realizer Foe Destroyers, abandoning the seeds of the conception of true existence is not the same as abandoning obstructions to omniscience.

Obstructions in the form of predisposing latencies – to be distinguished from seeds of the conception of true existence – are posited by the Prasangika system as the obstructions to omniscience. These are not abandoned until one attains the eighth ground. Therefore, the [Svatantrika] presentation which posits conceptions of true existence as obstructions to omniscience is not asserted by the Prasangika system. The Svatantrikas also divide obstructions to omniscience into nine segments – small, middling, and great [with small, middling, and great of each of these three]. These are in turn abandoned by nine paths of meditation, the second ground and so forth [according to Svatantrika but not Prasangika]. I will elaborate on this later.

The second position, that a Bodhisattva gains the ability to leap over certain levels of meditative stabilization on the seventh ground, is also incorrect. 'Leaping over' signifies a disordering of stages, and there is no source showing that such a leap-over does not occur in meditative stabilization on the sixth ground and below but does on the seventh.

The third position, that a Bodhisattva outshines Hearers and

Solitary Realizers through intelligence because the wisdom of the seventh ground approaches the irreversible eighth ground, is also incorrect. This still does not eliminate the doubt as to the reason for saying that although Bodhisattvas cannot outshine Hearers and Solitary Realizers on the sixth ground and below through their realization, they can outshine them on the seventh ground. Therefore, this is like making the disputed subject itself into the reason.

In his commentary[67] [Jaya-ananda] explains that on the seventh ground a Bodhisattva thinks, 'I will engage in the paths,' and therefore exerts himself, but because the signs of doctrine, such as sutras, are not manifest [in the sense of his not needing to use words of doctrine], he has attained a path of signlessness. [Jaya-ananda] explains that since sixth grounders and below and Hearers and Solitary Realizers do not have this signlessness, Bodhisattvas outshine them in intelligence. However, the feature of outshining them here appears to be posited in terms of cognition of suchness.

My excellent lamas have said that this feature should be posited from the viewpoint of entering into and arising from suchness – the limit of reality. It will be explained in connection with the seventh ground that from there a Bodhisattva is able to enter into and rise from cessation – the limit of reality – in each mental instant whereas those on the lower grounds are unable to do so. This explanation is good because while practising with belief [on the paths of accumulation and preparation] it is not difficult in quick succession to enter into and rise from meditative stabilization on emptiness in which the mind and suchness have not become of one taste. However, when one is a Superior – when the mind and suchness have become like water placed in water – this type of entering and rising is extremely difficult to accomplish.

OBJECTION: When the features of the *first* ground are being explained, it is inappropriate to say that on the *seventh* ground Bodhisattvas outshine Hearers and Solitary Realizers through their intelligence.

ANSWER: The fault of confusing subject matter is not in-

curred because Chandrakirti's explanation of the first ground
and so forth is based on the *Sutra on the Ten Grounds,* which
clearly discriminates between a first grounder's outshining
Hearers and Solitary Realizers through his conventional mind
generation but not through an ultimate mind generation. In
order to clear away doubts on what ground a Bodhisattva
outshines them through his realization, the sutra says that it is
on the seventh ground. Since Chandrakirti states this explanation here in his *Supplement,* it should be known that [his pro-
cedure] is very appropriate.

6 Hinayanists Cognize Emptiness

The Meaning Established by These Teachings

This section has three parts, (1) the teaching in the *Sutra on the Ten Grounds* that Hearers and Solitary Realizers cognize the non-inherent existence of phenomena, (2) the sources proving this, and (3) dispelling objections to this teaching.

The Teaching in the Sutra on the Ten Grounds *that Hearers and Solitary Realizers Cognize the Non-Inherent Existence of Phenomena*

This section has two parts, (1) clarification of the thought of the commentator, Chandrakirti, and (2) showing that this is also the system of Shantideva's *Engaging in the Bodhisattva Deeds*.

Clarification of the Thought of the Commentator, Chandrakirti

The *Sutra on the Ten Grounds* explains that on the sixth ground and below Bodhisattvas are unable to outshine Hearers and Solitary Realizers by way of their realization. Through this passage one can clearly ascertain that there are also [some] Hearers and Solitary Realizers who know that phenomena do not inherently exist.

If Hearers and Solitary Realizers did not have this wisdom, then even those Bodhisattvas who generate the first ultimate mind [the first ground] would outshine them from the view-point of their realization. Hearers and Solitary Realizers would be like sages who depend on worldly paths, which have the aspect of [considering lower levels to be] gross and [higher levels to be] peaceful, and thereby become free from desire, with the exception of that for the level called 'Peak of Cyclic Existence'. This absurd similarity would follow from holding that Hearers and Solitary Realizers lack the knowledge that phenomena do not inherently exist.

In that case, Chandrakirti says, Hearers and Solitary Realizers – like the non-Buddhist Forders – would not have abandoned all afflictions related to the three realms as well as their seeds. This indicates that if one has not understood emptiness well and become familiar with it, one cannot remove the seeds of the afflictions. This is like the situation of those cultivating worldly paths, which have the aspect of grossness and peacefulness, [but are unable to remove the seeds of afflictions].

If you lack cognition of suchness, you will conceive the aggregates, such as forms, to exist truly. Your mind will thereby err, and you will consequently not cognize a fully qualified selflessness of persons. This is because you will not have overcome belief in the referent object of a mind misapprehending true existence in the aggregates that are themselves the bases of designating a self or person.

Chandrakirti's statement of this indicates that if the referent object of the conception of true existence with regard to the aggregates – the bases of designation of a person – is not disbelieved, then the referent object of the conception of the true existence of the person – the phenomenon designated – will not be disbelieved. Because the person will not be cognized as lacking true existence, a fully qualified selflessness of the person will not be realized.

It is very difficult to understand the meaning of these statements, and it appears that those relying on this system and on Shantideva's texts have not explained them well. Therefore, in order to come to a final interpretation, let us examine a doubt raised about this and discover how it is dispelled.

DOUBT: Valid cognition establishes the sixteen attributes of the four noble truths, such as impermanence, emptiness, and selflessness – with the latter two referring to a substantially existent or self-sufficient person's lack of being either the same as or a different entity from the mental and physical aggregates. One definitely can ascertain these with valid cognition, and when that happens, the main trainees of these paths will familiarize with them intensely. The reasoning proving yogic direct perception establishes that when this happens, the self-lessness of the person will be directly cognized. Thus, it is established that a path of seeing, a consciousness cognizing the selflessness of the person, abandons the artificial afflictions. When this is established, a path of meditation that is a familiarization with the selflessness of the person, which has already been directly seen, is established. Since the innate afflictions are also abandoned through the path of meditation, an extinction of all the contaminations of the afflictions is established. Therefore, even though emptiness is not cognized, all the subtle increasers of contaminations with respect to the three realms, as well as their seeds, can be abandoned. This is because the abandonment by the paths of seeing and meditation as just explained is the manner by which a supramundane path achieves abandonment. Therefore, paths that are meditations on the sixteen attributes of the four noble truths – impermanence and so forth – are capable of removing all afflictions.

ANSWER: I will explain. We do not deny that even though one has not found the view of suchness, one can ascertain the sixteen attributes, impermanence and so forth, with valid cognition. We also do not deny that the trainees of this path meditate on the meaning of the sixteen with great effort, or that through having done so they directly see the coarse self-lessness of the person, or that familiarization with what has been seen is impossible.

QUESTION: Then what do you say?

ANSWER: Such a path is not a fully qualified cognition of the personal selflessness. Therefore, we do not assert that such paths are paths of seeing or supramundane paths of meditation.

These paths cannot abandon the seeds to be abandoned either through the path of seeing or through the path of meditation.

Explanations that these are paths of seeing and of meditation, that these abandon the artificial and innate afflictions as well as their seeds, and that at their end one attains the state of a Foe Destroyer are systems that require interpretation. For instance, the Chittamatrins establish through valid cognition a refutation of partless particles, an external world composed of them, and a subject that is a different entity from such an external world. When the trainees who are to be tamed by this teaching familiarize with it over a long time, they see it directly and then engage in further familiarization with what they have seen. However, the Madhyamikas explain that when progress on the ten grounds and on the latter three paths [seeing, meditation, and no more learning] is presented in terms of such teaching, the presentation must be interpreted. Even if one meditates on the sixteen aspects of the four noble truths, such as impermanence, only cognition of the [subtle] personal selflessness as explained above is asserted as a path freeing one from the afflictions.

Asanga's *Compendium of Knowledge* explains that afflictions are abandoned through mental application of selflessness and that the remaining attributes are means of training the mind. Dharmakirti's *Commentary on (Dignaga's) 'Compendium on Valid Cognition' (Pramāṇavarttika)* explains it similarly:

> One is liberated through the view of emptiness
> The other meditations are for the sake of that.

Some Indians [Shantirakshita, Kamalashila, Jetari, Prajnakaragupta, and so forth][68] mistook the term, 'the view of emptiness', and asserted it to be a viewing consciousness cognizing suchness, but this is not so. It refers to the [coarse] view of emptiness of a substantially existent, or self-sufficient, person. Although such a path cannot abandon the seeds of the afflictions, it can temporarily stop manifest afflictions.

Our assertion must accord with the statement in the *Knowledges* [the Hinayana and Mahayana *Abhidharmas*] that meditation having the aspect of grossness and peacefulness, which is common to Buddhists and non-Buddhists, abandons the manifest afflictions of Nothingness [the next to highest level within cyclic existence] and below. Therefore, it goes without saying that a path consciousness realizing the non-substantial existence of the person can temporarily abandon manifest afflictions.

The afflictions referred to in the phrase 'abandon manifest afflictions' are those whose objects of observation and subjective aspects are explained in the Hinayana and Mahayana *Knowledges* [and not those involving the conception of inherent existence]. These paths cannot [even temporarily] abandon the manifest conception of true existence which the Prasangikas explain as an afflicted ignorance. These paths also cannot abandon view and non-view afflictions[69] that accord with the conception of true existence and differ from the mode of explanation in the Hinayana and Mahayana *Knowledges*.

Furthermore, although meditation having the aspect of grossness and peacefulness cannot abandon the manifest afflictions included within the level of the Peak of Cyclic Existence as explained in the *Knowledges*, these can be abandoned through familiarization with the paths cognizing the coarse selflessness of the person explained above.

These points clarify Chandrakirti's statements in his commentary[70] that paths which are said to be antidotes abandoning the afflictions but which lack a cognition of suchness are like paths having the aspect of grossness and peacefulness and incapable of abandoning all afflictions, as in the case of the non-Buddhists.

This is also the System of Shantideva's Engaging in the Bodhisattva Deeds

The great Conqueror Child Shantideva also asserts this. His *Engaging in the Bodhisattva Deeds* (IX. 41ab)[71] says [citing an objector's opinion]:

> One is liberated through seeing the truths,
> What then is the use of seeing emptiness?

Someone asks, 'Since one is liberated from the afflictions

through the paths perceiving the sixteen attributes of the four
noble truths, impermanence and so forth, one does not need to
perceive the emptiness of inherent existence in order to extinguish the afflictions.' In answer to this, Shantideva says
(IX. 41cd):

> Scripture says that without this path
> There can be no enlightenment.

It is said in scripture that without the path perceiving the
emptiness of inherent existence one cannot attain any of the
three enlightenments [of a Hearer, Solitary Realizer, or Buddha].

With respect to how this is taught in scripture, Prajnakaramati's great commentary on *Engaging in the Bodhisattva Deeds*
quotes a mother sutra *(Perfection of Wisdom Sutra)* which
explains that one who discriminates true existence is not
liberated and that all [levels of the path] from Stream Enterer
to Solitary Realizer – in the past, present, and future – are
attained in dependence on just this perfection of wisdom. Thus,
Shantideva is not just referring to the highest enlightenment.
Shantideva says (IX.45):

> The root of the teaching is monkhood, but even
> It is difficult, for those whose minds apprehend
> [Inherent existence] find it hard
> To pass away from suffering.

[The roots of the teaching are monks who have abandoned the
afflictions, that is, Foe Destroyers. Not to mention Buddhahood,
even such monkhood is difficult, that is, impossible, if the
wisdom realizing emptiness is not cultivated, because the conception of inherent existence prevents nirvana. The teaching
is both the verbal and the realized doctrine. Foe Destroyers
such as Kashyapa, Upali, Ananda, the sixteen Elders *(Sthāvira)*,
and the Foe Destroyers present during the collections of the
word are called the roots of the teaching because they under-
took, sustained, and increased the doctrine.][72] These four lines
teach that nirvana cannot be attained by means of a path having
a mode of apprehension that involves conceiving true existence.

Then, Shantideva says (IX.46ab):

'Through abandoning the afflictions there is liberation.'
Then, immediately thereafter [extinguishment] would occur.

The first line states the opponent's position which is that
through cultivating the paths of the sixteen attributes of the
four truths, impermanence and so forth, the afflictions are
abandoned and liberation is attained. At this point the debate
concerns whether liberation from the afflictions can be attained
by means of only the paths of the sixteen attributes of the four
noble truths, impermanence and so forth. That this is the
meaning here is also very clear from the earlier debate (IX.41):

One is liberated through seeing the truths,
What then is the use of seeing emptiness?
Scripture says that without this path
There can be no enlightenment.

Therefore, the former passage should in no way be interpreted
to mean, 'We assert that the paths of merely the sixteen
attributes of the four noble truths, impermanence and so forth,
can extinguish the afflictions, but they do not liberate one from
all suffering.'

The thought of Shantideva's refutation is: The opponent
maintains that a liberation extinguishing the afflictions has
been attained when the afflictions that are also posited by the
two Hearer schools are not manifestly active due to generating
in the mental continuum the paths of the four truths. If so,
then immediately after having temporarily abandoned only
the manifest afflictions, a liberation extinguishing all con-
tamination would be attained.

Shantideva indicates that this cannot be asserted (IX.46cd):

Though [manifest] afflictions are [temporarily] absent
They are seen to have [rebirth by] the power of actions.

Though the manifest afflictions are temporarily absent, [such
persons] are seen to have the power impelling a future rebirth
through the force of contaminated actions *(karma)*.

These passages should be explained in this way and not as other commentators and some Tibetans have done, saying, 'Though they had no afflictions Maudgalyayana, Angulimala, and so forth were seen to have suffered from the effects of contaminated actions accumulated earlier when they were common beings; therefore, they were not immediately liberated.' Shantideva is not referring to [karmic] power that generates suffering in this lifetime. His passage must be understood as indicating that since the power of impelling a future rebirth through the force of contaminated actions has not been overcome, there is no liberation. For, Shantideva says (IX. 49abc):

Though an [afflicted] mind lacking [meditation on]
Emptiness is halted, it is again produced as in
The case of the absorption of non-discrimination.

If one lacks cognition of emptiness, then even though afflicted minds are temporarily halted through cultivating other paths, they cannot be totally overcome. Manifest afflictions are again produced, and thereby wandering in cyclic existence under the power of contaminated actions is not eliminated. That afflicted minds can be halted temporarily means, as was explained before, that manifest afflictions can be temporarily abandoned.

In answer to the statement, 'They are seen to have [rebirth by] the power of actions,' the opponent says (IX.47ab):

The absence of attachment
To rebirth is definite.

'Since these paths extinguish attachment that causes rebirth, it is certain that they will not be reborn again through the power of actions.' In answer to this, Shantideva says (IX.47cd):

This attachment is not afflicted but
Why is it not like obscuration?

The opponent asserts two types of ignorant obscuration – an afflicted and an unafflicted one as explained in the *Knowledges*.

Why not also assert afflicted and unafflicted attachment to accord with the explanation in the *Knowledges* [of those obscurations]? This indicates the existence of an 'unafflicted attachment' as it is commonly known in the two Hearer schools and in the Mahayana, but in our own [uncommon] system this attachment is said to be afflicted [because it is induced by the conception of inherent existence which is asserted as the chief affliction]. Therefore, the meaning of this passage is: Although the manifest [coarse] attachment induced by the conception of the person as substantially existent or self-sufficient has been temporarily abandoned, why is there no [subtle] attachment induced by the [subtle] view of the transitory collection – the conception that the person inherently exists?

One who has abandoned such [coarse] manifest afflictions has not even overcome the manifest [subtle] view of the transitory and manifest [subtle] attachment. If one has abandoned [only] the manifest afflictions of both these systems [Prasangika and non-Prasangika], the seeds of both [the coarse and subtle afflictions] have similarly not been abandoned, and if the manifest and non-manifest do not differ [as to whether or not their seeds have been abandoned], then it is senseless to differentiate attachments [by calling one afflicted and the other not because the afflictions have to be abandoned, both in manifest and seed form, for a person to become a Foe Destroyer].

Shantideva gives the reason why one who has abandoned other manifest [coarse] afflictions through other paths has not overcome [subtle] attachment (IX.48ab):

Attachment occurs through the cause
Of feeling, and they have feeling.

If one lacks the view cognizing suchness, then ignorance – the conception that feelings truly exist – is not in the least abandoned. Thus, when a feeling of pleasure is produced, why would attachment to not being separated from it not be generated? Also, when a feeling of suffering is produced, why would attachment wishing to separate from it not be generated? An effect is necessarily produced from causes with respect to which the favourable circumstances are complete and the unfavourable ones are absent.

According to our own system, the way to overcome attachment to feeling is expressed by Shantideva in his *Engaging in the Bodhisattva Deeds* (IX.99):

> When [it is seen] that there is no
> Feeler and feeling, why would
> Attachment not be overcome
> Through seeing this situation?

If one cultivates the perception that feeler and feeling do not at all inherently exist, one will overcome attachment. Shantideva is also indicating, 'If one does not have such a path, how could all attachment be overcome?' This is what Nagarjuna means when he says in his *Sixty Stanzas of Reasoning*:

> How could the great poison of the afflictions
> Not arise for one whose mind has a base?

Cha-ba (Rigs-pa'i-dbang-phyug Cha-pa-chos-kyi-seng-ge)[73] and Tsek-wang-chuk-seng-gay (rTsegs-dbang-phyug-seng-ge) refute Shantideva's *Engaging in the Bodhisattva Deeds*: 'Shantideva's explanation that attachment exists because feeling does is not good because the presence of a cause cannot prove that of an effect.' [ANSWER:] Of the two positions, that Hearers cognize the selflessness of phenomena and that they do not, the latter is well known in Tibet [even though it is wrong]. Being more accustomed to that system and not having trained decisively in the scriptures and reasonings of the former position, these commentators have not discerned the detailed meaning of the complete reasoning. They err greatly in rushing to impute fault to the great wise Shantideva.

Similarly, some Tibetans [Bu-tön, Pan-chen Jom-rel, and so forth][74] find fault with the honourable Chandrakirti; they express spurious faults without having any detailed understanding of their opponent's position [that is, Chandrakirti's

position that Hearers cognize the selflessness of phenomena].
Thus, when the wise see them illustrating their own nature,
it is only a source of extreme embarrassment.

In his commentary[75] [Jaya-ananda] says that the artificial
afflictions can be abandoned through the sixteen paths of the
four noble truths, impermanence and so forth, but not the
innate afflictions. This difference is not correct. With respect
to temporarily abandoning only the manifest [coarse] afflictions commonly spoken of in the vehicles, both the artificial
and the innate [coarse] afflictions are similar [in that the manifest forms of both can be temporarily abandoned through the
paths of the sixteen attributes of the four noble truths]. These
afflictions are also similar in that their seeds cannot be abandoned [by the paths of the four noble truths]. Here [Jaya-
ananda] does not know how to explain that Chandrakirti and
Shantideva are in agreement.

If one does not cognize the mental and physical aggregates
as not truly existing, then one will not cognize the person as
not truly existing and, thereby, will not cognize the selflessness
of the person. Just as the emptiness of true existence with
respect to phenomena such as the mental and physical aggregates is posited as the selflessness of phenomena, so the non-
true existence of the person should be put as the selflessness of
the person because the reasons [for doing so] are completely
similar [since non-true existence is the mode of being of both].

Because a conception that the person truly exists must be
posited as a conception of a self of persons, it is impossible to
extinguish all afflictions until that has been extinguished. Thus,
conceptions of the true existence of persons and phenomena
must be posited as afflictions. This very position must also be
presented in connection with Shantideva's system.

7 Liberation Is Impossible Without Wisdom of Emptiness

Sources Proving Hearers' and Solitary Realizers' Cognition of the Non-Inherent Existence of Phenomena

This section has two parts, sources (1) in Mahayana sutras and (2) in treatises and Hinayana sutras.

Sources in Mahayana Sutras Proving Hearers' and Solitary Realizers' Cognition of the Non-Inherent Existence of Phenomena

Chandrakirti quotes the *Questions of Adhyashaya Sutra* in his *Clear Words* [commenting on Nagarjuna's *Treatise on the Middle Way,* XXIII.14]:

> 'For example, during a magical display, a man sees a woman created by a magician and desire arises in him. His mind becomes ensnared with desire, and he is frightened and ashamed in front of his companions. Rising from his seat he leaves and later considers the woman to be ugly, impermanent, miserable, empty, and selfless. O child of good lineage, what do you think? Is that man behaving correctly or wrongly?'
>
> 'Blessed One, he who strives to consider a non-existent woman to be ugly, impermanent, miserable, empty, and selfless is wrong.'
>
> The Blessed One said, 'O child of good lineage, you should view similarly those monks, nuns, laymen and laywomen who consider unproduced and unarisen phenomena to be ugly,

F

impermanent, miserable, empty, and selfless. I do not say that these stupid persons are cultivating the path, they are practising wrongly.'

Thus, it was said very clearly [that those who conceive true existence are not liberated]. The example is the taking of a woman created by a magician as real and the subsequent consideration of her as impermanent and so forth. This should be understood as referring to conceiving that the aggregates truly exist and subsequently considering them to have the five qualities of impermanence and so forth.

This is a case of observing truly existent aggregates and considering them to be impermanent and so forth, and such consideration is only a wrong consciousness, mistaken with respect to its referent object [truly existent impermanent aggregates which actually do not exist]. Therefore, such is not validly established.

However, in the mental continuum of one who has not found the view overcoming belief in the object of the conception of true existence, there are many cases of observing aggregates that are not qualified by either truth or falsity and of establishing by conventional valid cognition that the aggregates have an impermanence and so forth which are not qualified by either truth or falsity. Also, paths, as explained before [in connection with the sixteen attributes of the four noble truths], are generated in the mental continuum during meditation through having meditated on the meaning [of impermanence and so forth without understanding non-true existence or positing true existence].

Also, in the *Sutra on the Miserliness of One in Trance (Dhyā-yitamuṣhṭi)*, which is quoted in [the twenty-fourth chapter of] Chandrakirti's *Clear Words*, Buddha says, 'Manjushri, sentient beings, whose minds are mistaken due to four errors through not seeing the noble truths correctly as they are in reality, do not pass beyond this unreal cyclic existence.' Manjushri responds, 'Blessed One, please indicate what is apprehended by sentient beings that causes them not to pass beyond cyclic existence.'

The Teacher said that sentient beings are not liberated because they do not know the four truths as they are in reality, and Manjushri requested Buddha to explain what is misconceived by sentient beings that causes them not to be liberated from cyclic existence. In answer to this, Buddha says that they think, 'I will pass beyond cyclic existence, and I will attain nirvana,' with a sense of adhering to the true existence of these. Therefore, when they have meditated on impermanence and so forth, they think, 'I know suffering, I have abandoned its sources, I have actualized its cessation, I have cultivated the path.' They then think, 'I have become a Foe Destroyer.' When they have temporarily abandoned the manifest afflictions explained above, they think, 'I have extinguished all contaminations.'

It is said that at the time of death they perceive that they will be reborn; thereby, they doubt Buddha, and this fault causes them to fall into a great hell. This applies to some who abide on such a path but not to all.

Then Manjushri asks how the four noble truths should be cognized since Buddha said that in order to liberate oneself from cyclic existence these truths must be known as they are in reality. In answer to this, Buddha says, 'Manjushri, he who sees all products as not produced knows suffering thoroughly. He who sees all phenomena as sourceless has abandoned the sources of suffering. He who sees them as utterly passed beyond sorrow has actualized cessation. He who sees all phenomena as totally unproduced has cultivated the path.' Then Buddha says that through this path one passes beyond sorrow without taking [rebirth].

This shows very clearly that one who sees the non-inherent existence of the four truths is liberated from cyclic existence and that one cannot be freed through a path unless it is devoid of the conception of true existence. This thereby indicates that the seeds of the afflictions cannot be abandoned through a path of only the sixteen attributes of the four noble truths, impermanence and so forth. It also shows that in order to abandon the seeds of the afflictions one must cognize the mode of being [of persons and other phenomena] and meditate on it.

If you do not distinguish these points well, you will hold that Hearers' paths for abandoning afflictions consist merely of meditation on the sixteen attributes of impermanence and so forth and that, therefore, Hearer Superiors and Foe Destroyers could not actually function as Superiors and Foe Destroyers. You would accumulate the great taint of deprecating Superiors, and if you have taken the Bodhisattva vow, this will produce a basic infraction. Shantideva's *Compendium of Instructions* sets forth this basic infraction:

> Holding that the Vehicle of Learners
> Does not abandon desire and so forth
> And causing others to believe the same. . . .

This meaning is also clearly set forth in the *Diamond Cutter Sutra (Vajrachchhedikā)*, ' "Subhuti, does a Stream Enterer think, 'I have attained the fruit of a Stream Enterer?" Subhuti answers, "Blessed One, it is not so. Why? Blessed One, he is called a Stream Enterer because he has not entered anything." '
Also, ' "Blessed One, if a Stream Enterer thought, 'I have attained the fruit of a Stream Enterer,' he would be conceiving a self of [himself and the fruit attained]. He would be conceiving a sentient being, a living being, and a person." '
Subhuti speaks likewise with respect to the latter three abiders in the fruits [of a Once Returner, Never Returner, and Foe Destroyer].

If through conceiving the attainer of the level of Stream Enterer and the fruit attained to exist truly, he thought, 'I have attained Stream Enterer,' he would be conceiving a self of those. Thus, it is said that conceptions of the true existence of the person and of the fruit are both conceptions of self – the first being a conception of a self of persons and the second of a self of phenomena.

That an [actual] Stream Enterer does not conceive the true existence of these and thereby think, 'I have attained the fruit,' refers to his having come to disbelieve the object of the conception of true existence.[76] Thus, this statement does not indicate that [at this early point in the path] he has no innate conception of true existence. On the basis of this it can be understood with respect to the later levels [that Once Returners, Never Returners, and Foe Destroyers do not conceive the true existence of themselves as attainers or the fruits attained].

Some Svatantrika-Madhyamikas explain this passage differently, but Prajnakaramati quotes it as a source showing that it is necessary to cognize emptiness to progress to the Hearer and Solitary Realizer enlightenment. His interpretation is good.

These scriptures only teach that if you lack the view of suchness, you cannot be freed from cyclic existence and that to be free this view is needed. No scholar asserts that Hearer and Solitary Realizer Foe Destroyers are not liberated from the fetters of cyclic existence; and furthermore, such an assertion is not feasible. Thus, these scriptures clearly teach that Hearers and Solitary Realizers cognize the non-inherent existence of phenomena.

There are many other sources such as the great mother *Perfection of Wisdom Sutras* and so forth, but fearing too many words, I will not cite them.

Sources in Treatises and in Hinayana Sutras

Nagarjuna's *Precious Garland* (35–37) says:

> As long as the aggregates are [mis]conceived,
> So long is there [mis]conception of an 'I'.
> When this conception of an 'I' exists,
> There is action which results in birth.

> With these three pathways in mutual causation
> Without a beginning, middle, or an end
> This wheel of cyclic existence
> Turns like the 'wheel' of a firebrand.

> Because this wheel is not obtained from self, other,
> Or from both in the past, the present, or the future,
> The conception of an 'I' ceases
> And thereby action and rebirth.

The first two lines teach that as long as there is a conception of the true existence of mental and physical aggregates, a view arises of the transitory collection which conceives a truly existent 'I'. This indicates that in order to extinguish the view of the transitory completely, it is necessary to extinguish the conception that the mental and physical aggregates truly exist. On this basis it can be known that Hearer and Solitary Realizer Foe Destroyers also totally abandon the conception that the aggregates truly exist.

Since the referent object of the view of the transitory is not disbelieved until the referent object of the conception of true existence is disbelieved, the personal selflessness known in both Hinayana and Mahayana schools of tenets is a refutation of only a coarse self of persons. It should be understood that this is not the subtle selflessness of persons.

Some hold that in the master Chandrakirti's system Hearers and Solitary Realizers cognize a selflessness of persons which is similar to that of the other schools. They thereupon propound a difference between Hearers and Solitary Realizers in that Hearers do not cognize the [coarse] selflessness of phenomena whereas Solitary Realizers do. They have not understood Chandrakirti's system well because his commentary[77] says that those who lack the view of suchness could not even realize the selflessness of persons.

The next two lines of Nagarjuna's *Precious Garland* teach that due to the presence of the view of the transitory as real 'I' and 'mine', actions binding one to cyclic existence are accumulated and through the force of these actions one is born in cyclic existence. This is said in terms of someone who has not come to disbelieve the referent object of the conception that the mental and physical aggregates truly exist. This is not applicable in general to one who merely possesses the view of the transitory as real 'I' and 'mine' because this view is present through the seventh ground, but from the first ground a Bodhisattva does not take rebirth by the power of contaminated actions.

These passages indicate that if you lack cultivation of the view of suchness, you cannot extinguish the view of the transitory as real 'I' and 'mine'. If you have no [practices] other than the paths of the sixteen attributes of the four truths, impermanence and so forth, the afflictions cannot be completely abandoned. Thus, once an uncommon selflessness of persons [their non-inherent existence] is posited, it would be a great mistake to leave as it is the presentation of the afflictions – identifying the view of the transitory as real 'I' and 'mine' and so forth in accordance with only the common selflessness of persons [their non-substantial existence]. One would not have delineated this uncommon system of tenets. How could this king of wise men [Chandrakirti] be mistaken about this?

Some of Chandrakirti's followers do not understand that he established this [Prasangika] system explaining that Hearers and Solitary Realizers cognize the selflessness of phenomena. Such followers do not even generate a thought wondering whether or not he has an uncommon way of positing the afflictions; they merely have faith in his 'system'. Using this as an example, you should examine well many other such occurrences.

The three pathways [mentioned in the quote from the *Precious Garland*] are the three sets of thorough afflictions – affliction [ignorance, attachment, and grasping], action [compositional action and 'existence'] and production [the other seven of the twelve links of dependent-arising: consciousness, name and form, six sources, contact, feeling, birth, and ageing and death]. These three pathways have no beginning, middle, or end. Actions arise from afflictions, and sufferings from actions; from sufferings arise sufferings similar in type as well as afflictions and so forth. Because these mutually produce each other, their order is indefinite. This is the meaning of their mutually causing each other.

This dependent-arising [of cyclic existence] is not produced from itself, from other, or from both self and other. Furthermore, inherently existent production is not obtained – that is to say, is not seen – in the past, present, or future. For this reason, wandering in cyclic existence is overcome through ex-

tinguishing the view of the transitory which conceives a real
'I'.

After that passage, Nagarjuna settles the selflessness of the
aggregates, constituents, and so forth, at the end of which he
says (365):

> Knowing thus truly and correctly
> That animate beings are unreal,
> Not being subject [to rebirth] and without grasping,
> One passes [from pain] like a fire without its cause.

Having seen suchness, one passes beyond suffering.

OBJECTION: Nagarjuna is speaking of seeing suchness only
in terms of Bodhisattvas.

ANSWER: Nagarjuna is speaking in terms of Hearers and
Solitary Realizers because right after that he says (366):

> Bodhisattvas *also* who have seen it thus,
> Seek perfect enlightenment with certainty,
> They maintain a continuity of existence
> Until enlightenment only through their compassion.

The passages from Nagarjuna's *Precious Garland* quoted by
Chandrakirti in his commentary were not rendered well in the
old translations.

In a sutra for Hearers, products are analysed as not existing
inherently by means of five examples in order that Hearers
might abandon the obstructions to liberation:[78]

> Forms are like balls of foam,
> Feelings are like bubbles,
> Discriminations are like mirages,
> Compositional factors are like banana trees,
> Consciousnesses are like magical illusions.
> Thus [the Buddha] the Sun-Friend said.

In his *Essay on the Mind of Enlightenment (Bodhichittavivaraṇa)*
Nagarjuna distinguishes between Hearers and Bodhisattvas:
'The Teacher taught the five aggregates for Hearers and the
five similarities – that forms are like balls of foam and so forth –
for Bodhisattvas.' His distinction is based on Hearers who are

temporarily unable to cognize suchness and does not refer to all Hearers. The same text says:

> Those who know not emptiness
> Are not bases for liberation.
> The obscured wander in the six migrations
> In the prison of cyclic existence.

Just this meaning of the non-inherent existence of phenomena is taught in the Hinayana scriptural divisions. Nagarjuna's *Precious Garland* (386) says:

> The teaching in the Mahayana of non-production
> And of extinction in the Hinayana are the same
> Emptiness [since they show that inherent existence] is extinguished
> And that nothing [inherently existent] is produced;
> Thus let the Mahayana be accepted [as Buddha's word].

Mahayana sutras teach an emptiness that is the non-existence of inherently existent production whereas when Hinayana sutras speak of emptiness, they teach an extinguishment of products. Both mean the same thing. Thus, do not be impatient with the teaching of emptiness in the Mahayana.

In what way do these two teachings have the same meaning? Some say, 'Hearers assert an extinguishment of products, but if products inherently existed, then that would not be feasible. Therefore, when an extinguishment of products is asserted, it is necessary to assert non-inherent existence from the beginning. Thus, these two teachings have the same meaning.'

This is very wrong. If that were so, then a sprout or any other phenomenon which the Madhyamikas assert to exist would have that reason; and, therefore, it would absurdly follow that sprouts, as well as all other products, and emptiness would be synonymous.

Also [Ajitamitra's] *Commentary on the Precious Garland* (*Ratnāvalīṭīkā*) says that there is no difference in meaning at all between non-production and momentariness. However, this is the explanation of one who has not understood the meaning of the text.

A Hinayana sutra [set forth by Shariputra after actualizing nirvana][79] quoted in Chandrakirti's *Commentary on (Nagarjuna's) 'Sixty Stanzas of Reasoning' (Yuktishashṭikāvṛtti)* says, 'Complete abandonment of these sufferings, definite abandonment, purification, extinguishment free from desire, cessation, thorough pacification, disappearance, non-connection to other suffering, non-arising, and non-production – this is peace, this is auspiciousness. It is like this: the definite abandonment of all the aggregates, the extinction of cyclic existence, freedom from desire, cessation, nirvana.' Commenting on this, Chandrakirti says that because the phrase 'these sufferings' uses the term of proximity 'these', the passage, 'Complete abandonment of all these sufferings . . . disappearance' refers only to the sufferings of aggregates that exist presently in one's own continuum. The passage 'non-connection to other suffering . . . nirvana' refers to future suffering. [Since this sutra clearly refers to the extinguishment of present suffering or the present mental and physical aggregates, it does not refer to an extinguishment brought about by the path but to the natural extinguishment which these phenomena have always had and which is seen in meditative equipoise.]

OBJECTION: 'Sufferings' and 'aggregates' are general terms used here for their instances, the afflictions. [Therefore, this sutra does not refer to an extinguishment of the aggregates in general.]

ANSWER: This also is not feasible. If general terms are not amenable to explanation with a general meaning, they must be explained as referring to their instances; here, however, this can be explained in the context of a generality. Otherwise, according to the proponents of true existence, a passage such as, 'The afflictions are primordially extinguished,' in Maitreya's *Sublime Science (Uttaratantra)* cannot be explained as primordial extinguishment in the sense that the aggregates have been primordially without inherently existent production. They must [incorrectly] explain this as a total abandonment by means of the path. Then, when the nirvana that is to be actualized exists, the actualizer would not [and thus could not report on the extinguishment that was realized, as was done in the sutra]. Also, when the actualizer exists, the nirvana to be actualized would not because the aggregates have not been extinguished. Thereby, they are unable to explain this sutra.

According to us, it is permissible to explain extinguishment here in accordance with the statement:

Extinguishment [in this case] is not [caused] by means of an antidote;
It is so called because of primordial extinguishment.

We are able to explain well the meaning of the sutra [as referring to a natural or primordial absence of inherent existence in phenomena].

A nirvana that is a cessation of suffering in the sense of a [primordial] extinguishment is taught in sutra, as well as a cessation in the sense of an absence of inherently existent production. The Superior Nagarjuna indicates that these are the same, and because his statement appears not to have been understood, I have explained it in detail.

Also, Nagarjuna's *Treatise on the Middle Way* (XV.7) says:

In the *Advice to Katyayana*
'Exists', 'not exists', and 'both'
Are rejected by the Blessed One
Knowing [the nature of]⁸⁰ things and non-things.

Thus, Nagarjuna teaches that a refutation of the two extremes is set forth in a Hinayana sutra, which appears in the *Brief Scriptures on Discipline (Vinayakshudravastu)*.

These are just illustrations. There are many [sources] in Nagarjuna's *Precious Garland* not quoted here, and many are also set forth in his *Sixty Stanzas of Reasoning* and *Collection of Praises*.

8 Distinction between Hinayana and Mahayana

Dispelling Objections to the Teaching that Hearers and Solitary Realizers Cognize the Non-Inherent Existence of Phenomena

This section has two parts, dispelling objections set forth in Chandrakirti's commentary and dispelling others not set forth there.

Dispelling Objections Set Forth in Chandrakirti's Commentary

Chandrakirti's commentary[81] sets forth [and then refutes] the position of the opponent, the [Svatantrika-Madhyamika] master Bhavaviveka, 'There is one who thinks, "If the selflessness of phenomena were taught in the Hearers' vehicle, then the teaching of Mahayana would be senseless." His system is to be understood as contradictory to reasoning and scripture.'

Buddhapalita, in his commentary on the seventh chapter of Nagarjuna's *Treatise on the Middle Way*, explains that Nagarjuna's statement that the selflessness of all phenomena is taught in Hinayana sutras refers to the non-inherent existence of phenomena. Bhavaviveka refutes this in his *Lamp for Wisdom*, 'If that were so, the Mahayana teaching would be senseless.'

Does Bhavaviveka mean that in general the Mahayana teaching would be senseless or that the Mahayana teaching of the selflessness of phenomena would be senseless? In the first case, if his consequence that the Mahayana teaching would be senseless follows from the reason that the selflessness of phenomena is taught in Hinayana, then the Mahayana teaching would be limited to teaching only the selflessness of pheno- mena. However, this is not so because Mahayana also teaches the Bodhisattva grounds, the practice of the perfections – giving and so forth – the great waves of aspirational prayers and dedications, great compassion as well as its accompanying topics, the great waves of the two collections, the marvellous power of the altruistic mind of enlightenment, and a reality inconceivable to common beings, Hearers, and Solitary Realizers [a Buddha's Truth Body]. Nagarjuna's *Precious Garland* (390, 393) says:

> Since all the aspirations, practices,
> And dedications of Bodhisattvas
> Were not explained in the Hearers' vehicle, how then
> Could one become a Bodhisattva through its path?

> The subjects based on the deeds of Bodhisattvas
> Were not mentioned in the [Hinayana] sutras
> But were explained in the Mahayana, thus
> The clear-sighted should accept it [as Buddha's word].

These stanzas were set forth to clear away the wrong idea: 'One can progress to Buddhahood through just the paths ex- plained in the scriptural divisions of the Hearers; therefore, the Mahayana is not needed.'

Chandrakirti is saying that according to Bhavaviveka Nagarjuna should have said, 'Because the selflessness of pheno- mena is set forth in the Mahayana, the explanations in the Hinayana scriptures are not sufficient [for the attainment of Buddhahood].' However, Nagarjuna did not say this but referred to other factors of the vast [methods of the Mahayana].

Bhavaviveka may mean that it would be senseless for the Mahayana to teach the selflessness of phenomena because it is taught in the Hinayana. This does not follow, however, be- cause the selflessness of phenomena is taught no more than briefly in the scriptural collections of the Hearers whereas it is taught very extensively from many viewpoints in the Mahayana. This also is the thought of the Superior Nagarjuna whose *Praise of the Supramundane (Lokātītastava)* says:

> You have said that without cognizing
> Signlessness, liberation[82] does not occur.
> Thus you taught it fully
> In the Mahayana.

The first two lines indicate that without cognizing suchness – signlessness – the afflictions cannot be extinguished and, therefore, liberation cannot be attained. The next two lines indicate that Buddha taught the selflessness of phenomena – signlessness – fully or completely in the Mahayana. Therefore, you should understand that the selflessness of phenomena was not fully taught in the Hinayana.

QUESTION: How does the reason given in [the first two lines of] that stanza explain why the selflessness of phenomena was taught fully in the Mahayana?

ANSWER: The liberation that is an extinguishment of the afflictions cannot be attained without cognizing signlessness; therefore, the selflessness of phenomena must also be taught in the Hearers' vehicle. For this reason, a difference between Hinayana and Mahayana [is that the selflessness of phenomena is set forth *fully* in the Mahayana]. This is how the reason should be interpreted.

Bhavaviveka's consequence [that the Mahayana teaching would be senseless], stated for the sake of refutation, and the opposite implied by that consequence [that the Hinayana does not teach the selflessness of phenomena] are thus shown to be facsimiles of refutation in which the pervasion is indefinite. In this way Bhavaviveka's refutation contradicts reasoning. The contradiction with scripture has been explained in detail above.

QUESTION: What is the meaning of the master Nagarjuna's explanation that the selflessness of phenomena is taught fully in the Mahayana but not in the Hinayana scriptures? Also, what is the meaning of his explanation that the selflessness of phenomena is fully cultivated on the Mahayana but not on the Hinayana path?

ANSWER: In no way does Nagarjuna teach that Hearers and Solitary Realizers do not, like the Mahayanists, cognize that all objects of knowledge are without inherent existence, but rather cognize that just a portion of objects of knowledge are without inherent existence. If a selflessness of phenomena is established by valid cognition in terms of one phenomenon, then when you analyse whether or not another phenomenon inherently exists, you can realize its non-inherent existence on the basis of your previous reasoning.

Some who wish to be Madhyamikas assert a system refuting the true existence of phenomena but maintain that the emptiness of true existence truly exists, while others assert that a positive independent nature of phenomena truly exists. The former appears to have the fault of not delimiting well the measure of true existence and thereby of refuting only a coarse form of it. The latter claims to refute the true existence of phenomena but appears not to have done so through valid cognition and instead abides in a view that is a denial of phenomena. Therefore, these [two wrong interpretations] cannot challenge [our position that if the emptiness of one phenomenon is realized, the emptiness of any phenomenon can be realized based on the previous reasoning].

To establish that even a single phenomenon does not truly exist, Mahayanists use limitless different reasonings as set forth in the *Treatise on the Middle Way*. Hence their minds become greatly broadened with respect to suchness. Hinayanists use only brief reasoning to establish suchness by valid cognition, and since they do not establish emptiness the way Mahayanists do, do not have a mind broadened with respect to suchness. Therefore, Nagarjuna sets forth a difference of vastness or abbreviation and of fully or not full meditating on selflessness. This difference arises because Hearers and Solitary Realizers strive to abandon only the afflictions [the obstructions to liberation], and cognizing a mere abbreviation of the meaning of suchness is sufficient for that. Mahayanists are intent on abandoning the obstructions to omniscience, and for that it is necessary to have a very broadened mind of wisdom opened to suchness.

Dispelling Objections Not Set Forth in Chandrakirti's Commentary

OBJECTION: Maitreya's *Ornament for the Realizations* says:

> Know that the paths of the rhinoceros-like
> Are included completely within
> Abandonment of the thought of an object,
> Non-abandonment of a subject, and the base.

Thus, Maitreya says that through the paths of a Solitary Realizer one is able to abandon thought adhering to the truth of an object but not adherence to the truth of a subject. Maitreya also says:

> Due to diminishment of the afflictions,
> Objects of knowledge, and the three paths
> There are purities of the students,
> The rhinoceros-like, and Conqueror Children.[83]

How do you interpret Maitreya's saying that adherence to the truth of objects is an obstruction to omniscience?

ANSWER: The meaning of Solitary Realizers' abandoning adherence to external objects must be interpreted in one of two ways:

1 Though external objects are established by valid cognition, Solitary Realizers meditate on the meaning of a reasoned refutation of the true existence of external objects, as laid down by the Madhyamikas. They thereby abandon adherence to the truth of external objects.
2 On the basis of having meditated on the meaning of a reasoned refutation of external objects in accordance with Chittamatra, Solitary Realizers abandon the conception that external objects exist.

The first interpretation is wrong. If one who can posit the general existence of external objects refutes their true existence through a reasoning analysing suchness, then, when he analyses whether subjects truly exist, he can – based on the force of the former reasoning – realize that subjects do not truly exist. Aryadeva's *Four Hundred* says:

> He who sees the suchness of one phenomenon
> Sees the suchness of all phenomena.

[Therefore, it would be impossible to abandon the conception that objects truly exist without forsaking the conception that subjects so exist.]

Commentaries by [Svatantrika-Madhyamika] masters such as Haribhadra assert the meaning of this passage from Maitreya's *Ornament for the Realizations* in accordance with the second intrepretation. For them valid cognition establishes that external objects do not exist. Once this has been established, then anyone – even with dull faculties – would understand that a consciousness apprehending an object is not a different entity from its object. Therefore, Maitreya's statement that Solitary Realizers do not abandon adherence to the truth of subjects should be understood as the [Solitary Realizers'] general assertion that minds truly exist. In no way could they refute [the true existence of] one half of subject and object which are different entities and conceive of the truth of the other half. Therefore, the statement that it would be amazing to have a similarity of tenet between the Solitary Realizers who compound the truth of subjects and the Chittamatrins who teach the ultimate existence of a consciousness without the duality of subject and object is laughable even for the non-Buddhist Dipakas.

[In the Yogachara-Svatantrika system] the path of a Solitary Realizer is said to be middling from the viewpoint of his abandoning adherence to the truth of objects [which are different entities from their subjects] and his not abandoning adherence to the true existence of subjects. Through abandoning adherence to the truth of objects he is superior to a Hearer, and through not abandoning adherence to the truth of subjects he is inferior to a Mahayanist [who realizes the non-true existence of all phenomena]; therefore, he is middling.

[For the Yogachara-Svatantrikas] the three persons of the three vehicles – great, middling, and small – have sharp, middling, and dull faculties, and thus they posit stages of faculties in relation to selflessness. They posit the best, the Madhyamika view, for the great vehicle. They posit the middling view of Chittamatra for the middling vehicle, and the lowest view, the common one of the selflessness of the person, for the small vehicle. However, it is not definite [that this is the only way of positing a difference in faculty according to Haribhadra and so forth]. Even according to [a system propounding that] all three have the view of suchness, it is not contradictory that there be three stages of faculties from the viewpoint of [trainees'] quickly or not so quickly penetrating suchness, and so forth.

Maitreya teaches that the inability to abandon adherence to the truth of the subject – consciousness – is a distinguishing feature of the low vehicle. Therefore, it is not suitable to interpret the view of selflessness explained in his *Ornament for the Realizations* as Chittamatra, as is the case with his *Ornament for the Mahayana Sutras, Discrimination of the Middle Way and the Extremes (Madhyāntavibhaṅga)*, and *Discrimination of Phenomena and the Nature of Phenomena (Dharmadharmatāvibhaṅga)*. Even Indian [scholars] interpreted Maitreya's *Ornament for the Realizations* [variously] as Madhyamika and as Chittamatra, and their many reasons regarding this should be explained; however, fearing too many words I will not write about it now.

Furthermore, Maitreya's *Ornament for the Realizations* says:

> The element of qualities has no divisions
> Therefore the lineages cannot be different.
> Divisions of lineage are thoroughly imputed
> Through differences in the dependent phenomena.

This indicates that Hearers and Solitary Realizers also cognize the nature of phenomena. With respect to the term 'element of qualities' *(dharmadhātu)* Aryavimuktasena's *Illumination of the Twenty-Five Thousand Stanza Perfection of Wisdom (Pañchaviṃshatisāhasrikāprajñāpāramitopadeshashāstrābhisamayālaṃkā –*

ravṛtti) says, ' "Thought" and "conception" are an adherence
to phenomena and their signs. Because these do not exist,
desire is to be known as just non-existent. This non-existence is
the suchness of all phenomena. This indicates that the element
of qualities itself is the cause of the qualities of Superiors, and it
is thus the basis of achieving the natural lineage.' The element
of qualities is explained as the emptiness of true existence that
is the non-existence of phenomena and their signs as they are
apprehended by desire, which here refers to a consciousness
adhering to the true existence of phenomena and their signs.

An objection is stated: 'If the element of qualities were the
lineage, then all sentient beings would abide in the lineage
because the element of qualities in general would abide in all.'
The objector thinks that abiding in the lineage refers to the
lineage on the occasion of the path.

In answer to this it is said, 'The lineage is that which serves
as the cause of Superiors' qualities when observed; thus, here
the absurd consequence [that all sentient beings would have the
qualities of Superiors] is not entailed.' The mere presence of the
nature of phenomena does not mean that one abides in the
lineage in terms of the path. When one observes and meditates
on the nature of phenomena through the path, it comes to
serve as the special cause of Superiors' qualities. At that time
one's lineage is regarded as special.

An objection is raised, 'Still, since the element of qualities
has no divisions, the lineages of the three vehicles could not be
different.' In answer, it is said that because there are divisions
in the paths, which are dependent phenomena observing [the
element of qualities], the lineages are asserted to be different.

The basis [the element of qualities] is what is observed, and
the dependent are the consciousnesses observing it. With respect
to the observers, there are also the two vehicles of Hearers and
Solitary Realizers. In order for the element of qualities to be
observed, it must be established for that mind, and unless true
existence is eliminated for that mind, an emptiness of true
existence is not established for it. If emptiness is not established
for it, then neither is the nature of phenomena.

The fact that the nature of phenomena must be initially ascertained in relation to one [particular] base qualified by emptiness shows that Hearers and Solitary Realizers take cognizance of either an external or internal phenomenon qualified by emptiness and observe its nature – its non-true existence. Thus, there are Solitary Realizers who cognize the meaning of suchness, and it does not follow that no Solitary Realizer can abandon adherence to the truth of consciousnesses.

Also, Hearers must be divided into those who do and do not realize suchness, and for this reason two Hinayana modes were set forth in Maitreya's *Ornament for the Realizations*. You must ascertain that [in Maitreya's *Ornament for the Realizations* which contains two systems] conceptions of a true difference in entity of subject and object are both assigned and denied as obstructions to omniscience.

OBJECTION: The objection here is not that the lineages of the three vehicles could not be different but that a division into thirteen lineages is not feasible.

ANSWER: This is not correct. On this subject Maitreya's *Ornament for the Realizations* is similar to the statement of a hypothetical objection in Aryavimuktisena's *Illumination of the Twenty-Five Thousand Stanza Perfection of Wisdom Sutra*: 'As it is said in sutra, "Manjushri, if the element of qualities is one, if suchness is one, and if the limit of reality is one, then how could receptacles and non-receptacles be designated?" ' The question is that since it is said in other sutras that the element of qualities has no divisions, how could persons be designated as receptacles and non-receptacles of Mahayana? Since the objection in Maitreya's *Ornament for the Realizations* is similar to this, it is that the lineages of the greater and lesser vehicles could not be different. It does not refer to ascribing receptacles and non-receptacles in terms of thirteen lineages.

The assertions of the master Haribhadra also are similar to those of Aryavimuktisena. Likewise, Maitreya's *Sublime Science* and Asanga's commentary on it explain that among Hearers and Solitary Realizers there are some who have cognized the nature of phenomena and others

who have not. Fearing it would be too much, I will not cite
them.

How do we know there are these two types [Hinayanists
who have and have not cognized emptiness]? Maitreya's
Ornament for the Realizations teaches [a Bodhisattva's] path
knowledge which involves understanding the paths of Hearers
and Solitary Realizers so that a Bodhisattva can accommodate
[trainees] with those lineages. There are two types, those who
are and are not vessels of the profound [emptiness], and since
Hearers and Solitary Realizers are predominantly not vessels
of the profound, their paths were most frequently presented.
Just as with respect to Mahayana it sometimes happens that
unless one is taught Chittamatra first, one cannot find the
Madhyamika view, this is also the case with Solitary Realizers
and even Hearers. [Therefore, they are often not taught the
profound emptiness initially even though realization of it is
the only path of liberation.]

In both Aryavimuktisena's *Illumination of the Twenty-Five
Thousand Stanza Perfection of Wisdom Sutra* and Haribhadra's
*Great Commentary on the Eight Thousand Stanza Perfection of
Wisdom Sutra (Aṣṭasāhasrikāprajñāpāramitāvyākhyānābhisama-
yālaṃkārāloka)* the element of qualities is assigned as the lineage
of all three vehicles. As a source for this they quote the teaching
that all Superior persons are distinguished by the non-product
[the element of qualities, emptiness]. As a proof for the statement, 'The qualities of an enlightened one and all the doctrines
taught by him do not exist,' the *Diamond Cutter* says, 'Superior
persons are distinguished by the non-produced.' This means
that all Superiors of the greater and lesser vehicles are posited
by way of their having actualized the non-produced ultimate
which is the non-establishment of phenomena in reality.

Therefore, this [Prasangika] system and Maitreya's *Ornament for the Realizations* are not contradictory. You should
understand that the systems of the commentators on Maitreya's
Ornament for the Realizations also contain two modes.
Enough elaboration.

9 Perfection of Giving

Surpassing Feature on the First Ground

This section has four parts, the giving of abiders on the first ground, of those with a lower basis, of Bodhisattvas, and the divisions of the perfection of giving.

The Giving of Abiders on the First Ground

Chandrakirti says in his root text:

9ab   *Then for him the first cause of perfect*
      Enlightenment – giving – becomes surpassing.

When a Bodhisattva attains the Very Joyful Ground, the perfection of giving among the ten perfections becomes greatly surpassing for him. However, this does not mean that he does not have the other perfections. The supramundane perfection of giving is the first supramundane cause of complete enlightenment.

   In general the latter perfections exceed the former ones, but on the first ground it is said that giving is surpassing. This means that here a Bodhisattva has not developed the measure of force with respect to the practice of ethics and so forth that he has with respect to the practice of giving. As it is said, on the first ground he is able to practise it by giving away his own body and external belongings such that even the slightest attachment – which would be contrary to the perfection of giving – does not arise. On the second ground a Bodhisattva is able to refrain totally from faulty ethics – the contraries of proper ethics – even in dreams, but on the first ground he is not able to do so.

Through his giving, one can infer the presence of unimaginable realizations on the first ground; Chandrakirti's root text says:

9cd   *His devotion to giving even his own flesh*
       Is reason for inferring the unimaginable.

Not only does the Bodhisattva give external articles with enthusiasm, but he even has great enthusiasm for giving his own flesh to one who asks for it. This quality serves as the cause for inferring internal realizations – such as attaining a ground – which most other persons cannot imagine. The inference is similar to fire being inferred due to the presence of smoke, etc.

This indicates that the Bodhisattva has no taints of attachment with respect to giving away his body, life, and resources. Even though he gives these away, his continuum remains firm without changing its aspect.

The Giving of Those with a Lower Basis
This section has two parts, attaining the happiness of cyclic existence and of nirvana through giving.

Attaining the Happiness of Cyclic Existence Through Giving
Chandrakirti's root text says:

10   *All these beings want happiness, but human*
      Happiness does not occur without resources.
      Knowing that resources arise from giving,
      The Subduer first discoursed on that.

All these beings want to attain the happiness that is a diminishment of sufferings such as hunger, thirst, sickness, heat, and cold. However, the happiness of humans and so forth is not produced without their enjoying desired objects or resources, such as food, drink, means of curing sickness, clothing, and shelter. The Subduer, understanding the thought of all migrators and knowing that these resources arise from merit accu-

mulated by previous giving, discoursed on giving from the very
first for it is easy to engage in this method.

QUESTION: Must a giver accord with proper ways in order
to attain marvellous resources from giving gifts?

ANSWER: That is not necessary; Chandrakirti's root text says:

11   *Even for beings with little compassion,*
      Brutal and intent on their own aims,
      Desired resources arise from giving,
      Causing extinguishment of suffering.

There are those who, like merchants, seek to gain an enormous
mass of wealth by giving away very little. Wanting far vaster
resources than do even beggars, they are enthusiastic in giving.

As givers their compassion is low, and, unlike Bodhisattvas
under the influence of compassion, they do not seek to increase
the joy of wanting to give without seeking the fruits of giving.
Moreover, intent on only their own welfare – the happiness of
high status – their minds are extremely brutal toward sentient
beings. They have turned away from the fault of holding
on to resources and of not giving them away but anxiously
hold on to their sole hope which is for reward. Even for them,
giving serves as a cause of extinguishing the sufferings of hunger,
thirst and so forth by bringing marvellous resources.

Attaining the Happiness of Nirvana through Giving

Chandrakirti's root text says:

12   *Through giving even they will quickly attain*
      A meeting with a Superior Being.
      Then they will cut the continuum of cyclic existence,
      Going to the peace caused by meeting a Superior.

Even those bereft of compassion but intent on giving – looking
after only their own happiness in the sense of diminishing
suffering – quickly attain a meeting with a Superior Being
while they give. This is because the excellent are said to
associate with patrons, to whom they then teach doctrine.
Through this, the patrons come to understand cyclic existence

as being without any good features. Through actualizing uncontaminated superior paths, they abandon ignorance and
completely sever the continuum of cyclic existence – the
passage from birth to death again and again since beginningless
time. They pass to the peace of a Hearer's or Solitary Realizer's
nirvana which is caused by meeting with the excellent.

Bodhisattvas' Giving

This section has four parts, extraordinary benefits of Bodhisattvas' giving, the importance of discourse on giving for both the
compassionate and the non-compassionate, the joy attained by
Bodhisattvas when giving, and whether or not suffering occurs
when a Bodhisattva gives away his body.

Extraordinary Benefits of Bodhisattvas' Giving

Chandrakirti's root text says:

13ab *Those bearing in mind a promise to help beings*
      Attain happiness from giving before too long.

When non-Bodhisattvas satisfy a beggar through giving, it is
not definite that they at the time or immediately afterwards
enjoy the happiness that is the fruit of their giving. Because
non-Bodhisattvas do not at once see the fruit of their giving, it
even happens that [for this reason] they do not engage in giving.
However, Bodhisattvas, who bear in mind their promise to
help all migrators in the long run and to achieve happiness for
them temporarily, attain the fruit of their giving – a supreme
joy – as soon as they see a beggar's satisfaction. Enjoying the
fruits of giving, Bodhisattvas take joy in giving at all times.

Importance of Discourse on Giving for Both the Compassionate and the Non-Compassionate

Chandrakirti's root text says:

13cd *For those merciful and those not so*
      Only discourse on giving is therefore chief.

Giving induces the happiness of high status and definite good-

ness in the way explained above for all whose nature is mercy –
Bodhisattvas – and for all who do not have a nature of mercy.
Therefore, just discourse on giving is chief, that is to say, very
important.

Nagarjuna's *Friendly Letter* says:

> There is no better friend for the future
> Than giving – bestowing gifts properly
> On monks, brahmins, the poor, and friends – knowing
> Resources as evanescent and pithless.

The Joy Attained by Bodhisattvas When Giving

QUESTION: When Bodhisattvas satisfy beggars with enjoyments, what kind of joy is generated in them that causes their
enthusiasm for giving?

ANSWER: Chandrakirti's root text says:

14 *Whereas when a Conqueror Child hears and thinks*
    Of the word 'give', happiness arises,
    The subduers abiding in peace have no [such] happiness.
    What need is there to mention [the joy of] giving all?

When a Bodhisattva thinks of the meaning of the words heard
from beggars saying, 'Give,' he thinks, 'They are begging from
me,' and from this a happiness arises again and again in his
mind. Such happiness is not generated in the subduer Foe
Destroyers by abiding in the element of peace – nirvana. What
need is there to mention that happiness surpassing this peace is
generated by satisfying beggars through giving away all
external and internal phenomena?

If the mind is captivated by the peace of nirvana, one forgets
others' welfare. However, the captivation of a Bodhisattva's
mind by the happiness explained earlier causes him to strive
even harder for the welfare of others; therefore, this is a different type of happiness.

Whether or Not Suffering Occurs When a Bodhisattva Gives Away His Body

QUESTION: Is physical suffering experienced by Bodhisattvas

who give away external and internal phenomena and who are said to generate wonderful happiness from any giving?

ANSWER: If this question is asked in terms of great beings who have attained a ground, no physical suffering occurs, as is the case when mindless things are cut. The *Questions of Gaganaganja Sutra (Gaganagañjaparipṛchchhā)*[84] says, 'It is this way: There is, for instance, a grove of great *shāla*[85] trees, and when someone enters it and cuts down a tree, the remaining trees do not become desirous or angry thinking, "It was cut down, not us." They have no thought or imagination. Such patience in a Bodhisattva is the supreme thoroughly purified patience, equal to space.'

Also Nagarjuna's *Precious Garland* (226) says:

If his body does not suffer,
How can he suffer in mind?
Through great compassion he feels pain
For the world and so stays in it long.

Nagarjuna says this about those who have attained a ground.

If the question is asked in terms of those who have not attained the Very Joyful Ground in which there is no attachment to body and resources, then physical suffering definitely does arise since conditions contrary to sustaining the body befall it. However, suffering at that time only causes one to become more involved in the welfare of sentient beings. Chandrakirti's root text says:

15   *Through his own suffering in cutting and giving*
    Away his body, he sees with knowledge others' pain
    In hells and so forth, and strives quickly
    To eliminate their suffering.

A Bodhisattva understands the frightful state of migrators such as hell-beings, animals, and hungry ghosts. He sees that physically they are overwhelmed with great suffering which is without a break and thousands of times more unbearable than that of mutilating his own body. Through his own suffering – not considering what he suffered when he cut his body and gave it to a beggar, but because of that painful experience – he very quickly begins striving to eliminate the sufferings of other sentient beings in the hells and so forth. Nak-tso's translation of this stanza is:

> Through the suffering of cutting and giving away his body
> He views the pain of others in the hells and so forth,
> And from his own experience
> He strives to eliminate it.

My explanation depends on both translations.

If such power of thought is possessed, one can give away one's body. Since it is not contradictory for that thought to be present in Bodhisattvas who have not attained a ground, it is said that they also give away their bodies.

Divisions of the Perfection of Giving

Chandrakirti's root text says:

16ab *Giving void of gift, giver, and receiver*
      Is called a supramundane perfection.

The giving of one whose thought to give away is conjoined with the uncontaminated wisdom empty of observing gift, giver, and receiver as truly existent is called a supramundane perfection. This is said in *The Great Perfection of Wisdom*.

The unapprehendable meditative equipoise of a Superior is supramundane; therefore, giving conjoined with it is assigned as such a perfection. Giving that is not conjoined with this unapprehendability is mundane. The difference between them cannot be directly ascertained by those who have not attained an ultimate mind of enlightenment.

With respect to the term 'perfection' [or 'transcendence'], the beyond is the far shore or port of the ocean of cyclic existence – Buddhahood, the state of having abandoned the two obstructions without remainder. 'Transcend' means go beyond.

In his commentary Chandrakirti[86] says, 'By the rule, "The elision does not take place before the second member of the compound,"[87] the case of the object is not elided and therefore is manifest. Or, because [the compound is classed with] *pṛṣhodara* and so forth, [which are exceptional compounds,[88] the word *pārama*] is left with just an *m* ending.' The pandit Jaya-ananda explains the meaning of this as follows: In the language of India [Sanskrit] *pāra* means 'the farther side', and *itā* means 'gone'. When these two words are compounded, the accusative singular *am* is added to *pāra*, and the nominative ending *su* is added after *itā*; then, *pāram-itā* is compounded as *pāramitā*. Even though *am* and *su* are to be elided, *su* is elided but *am* is not because of the rule in the root grammar, 'The elision does not take place before the second compound [in some situations].'

Chandrakirti's reference to the 'case of the object' is to the accusative singular *am*. Since it is not elided, it is included in the final form of the term *pāramitā*.

In [this case of] '*pṛṣhodara* and so forth' the word *pārama* [is left] with an *m* ending. Because *pārama* is said, [the rule of] non-elision is cited.[89] The *a* of *ma*[90] is erased, leaving *m* to which *i* is added, making *mitā*. *Su* seems wrong as the nominative ending; thus, analysis is needed as to whether it should be *si*.[91]

There appear to be many explanations by Tibetans which are fabrications of darkness such as 'In the language of India "perfection" is *pāramitā* (*pāraṃ ita*); the anusvara is placed in file, and it becomes *pāram-ita*. When it is compounded, the vowel sign of *i* [over *a* as it is written in Tibetan] is added to *m*, and *a* is erased leaving *mitā*.' However, the pandit's explanation is that stated above.

These two lines in Chandrakirti's root text specify the wisdom cognizing the three spheres [of giver, gift, and receiver] to be unapprehendable [as inherently existent entities] and explain the specific perfection of giving which is conjoined with that wisdom. Giving and so forth that are not conjoined with this wisdom are *similar* to a perfection conjoined with wisdom and, therefore, are called 'perfections'. Although they are not conjoined with wisdom, they are conjoined with dedication to great enlightenment and, therefore, are posited as definite to go beyond. Thus, they gain the name of a perfection of giving.

When the meaning of 'perfection' is applied to the object – the beyond to which one goes – it refers to the Buddhahood to which one progresses. When it is taken as the means by which one goes beyond, perfections occur even on paths of learning. Through this explanation of giving, it should be understood that ethics and so forth can be conjoined with an altruistic mind of enlightenment, dedication, and wisdom – individually and collectively.

Chandrakirti's root text says:

16cd   *When attachment to these three is produced,*
       It is called a mundane perfection.

Sutra teaches that giving is called a mundane perfection when one is bound through having generated attachment, which is an adherence to the true existence of the three spheres of giving.

With respect to putting into practice now the features explained above, you should, through imagination, train in giving your own body to others and in the special ways of generating joy. You should continuously amass other forms of giving articles by giving away anything – from water on up – to lower and higher fields of giving. At that time your giving should be conjoined with the wisdom realizing the un-apprehendability of the three spheres [as inherently existent]. Furthermore, you should again and again give away in thought your own body, resources, and roots of virtue for the sake of sentient beings. You should consider that even if you do not give these away, they will disintegrate; thereby, you will have to lose them, and thus it would be better to give them first through your own thought as if you were actually giving them. Shantideva's *Engaging in the Bodhisattva Deeds* (III.10) says;

To accomplish all sentient beings'
Welfare, give away without regret
Body as well as resources and all
Virtues of past, present, and future.

Also (III. 11):

> Through giving away all one passes beyond sorrow,
> And one's intention is to achieve nirvana.
> Similar to losing all [at death], the best
> Is to give to sentient beings [now].

CONCLUSION BY WAY OF EXPRESSING THE FEATURES OF THE FIRST GROUND

Chandrakirti now sets forth the Very Joyful Ground, which was explained above, by summarizing the features of that ground as qualities of uncontaminated wisdom. His root text says:

17   *Abiding thus in the mind of a Child of a Conqueror*
   Beautifying with light this excellent base,
   The Joyful [Ground] like a water crystal jewel
   Destroys and overcomes all heavy darkness.'

The Very Joyful Ground abides like the orb of the moon – the water crystal jewel.

The first ground is similar to the moon in three ways. One is its abiding in a high place. Because the first ground abides in the mind of a first grounder – a Conqueror Child who has attained the features of that ground as explained earlier – it abides on a high path and thereby is similar to the moon high up in the sky. Since the first ground is part of a Bodhisattva's mind, it is said to abide in his mind, like an eye in the head.

His mind – the excellent or superior base in which the ultimate mind of the first ground abides – is made beautiful by the light of wisdom; therefore, the first ground is similar to the moon beautifying the sky – its base – with white light. Also, because the first ground abides overcoming what is unfavourable to it – that which is to be abandoned through the path of seeing – it is like the moon destroying all heavy darkness.

Such is the explanation of the first ultimate mind generation in the *Illumination of the Thought, an Extensive Explanation of Chandrakirti's 'Supplement to the Middle Way.'*

10   Perfection of Ethics

SECOND GROUND, THE STAINLESS

This section has five parts, thorough purification of ethics on the second ground, praise of ethics, example of non-mixture with what is not conducive to ethics, divisions of the perfection of ethics, and conclusion by way of expressing the features of the second ground.

THOROUGH PURIFICATION OF ETHICS ON THE SECOND GROUND

This section has four parts, sublimity of ethics on the second ground, thorough purification of features in dependence on ethics, their superiority on the second ground over the first, and another cause of their thorough purification.

Sublimity of Ethics on the Second Ground

Chandrakirti's root text says:

18ab   *Because his ethics are sublime and have pure qualities,*
       He forsakes the stains of faulty ethics even while he dreams.

Because one who abides on the second ground possesses very sublime ethics and pure qualities, he forsakes, or is not polluted by, the stains of faulty ethics not only when awake but also when dreaming.

This does not refer merely to faulty ethics in the sense of root infractions and transgressions of natural codes but signifies that he has abandoned the stains of all faulty ethics, even those which are transgressions of formulated codes.

[Having] 'proper ethics' (*shīla*) means that one does not assume afflictions which motivate faulty ethics and that sinful actions discordant with formulated codes do not arise. Thereby, one has extinguished the fire of contrition for the arising of infractions discordant with formulated codes and has thus attained a coolness. The Sanskrit original of 'proper ethics' is *shīla*. *Shīta* means 'cool'; *lāti* means 'attained'. Another explanation is that proper ethics (*shīla*) is so called because, due to its being a cause of happiness, it is taught by the excellent. These are contextual etymologies [with letters added].

From the viewpoint of its entity, proper ethics has the character of seven abandonments – abandoning the seven faulty modes of body and speech [killing, stealing, sexual misconduct, lying, divisive talk, harsh speech, and senseless chatter]. The motivators of the seven abandonments are non-covetousness which is non-desire, non-harmfulness which is non-hatred, and right view which is freedom from wrong views. Therefore, in terms of its entities as well as its motivators, proper ethics is comprised of the ten abandonments – the paths of wholesome actions abandoning the ten paths of unwholesome actions.

Thorough Purification of Features in Dependence on Ethics

QUESTION: How do a Bodhisattva's qualities become pure through the sublimity of his ethics?

ANSWER: Chandrakirti's root text says:

18cd   *Because his movements of body, speech, and mind are pure,*
           He accumulates all ten paths of excellent deeds.

On all occasions of waking and dreaming his movements or activities of body, speech, and mind are pure of even subtle infractions; therefore, he accumulates all ten paths of excellent or supreme deeds. His accumulation of these means that he fulfills the first three paths of virtuous actions – abandoning killing,
G

stealing, and sexual misconduct – with his body; the middle four – abandoning lying, divisive talk, harsh speech, and senseless chatter – with his speech; and the last three – abandoning covetousness, harmful intent, and wrong views – with his mind. Not only does he refrain from what is prohibited but also he fulfills all the positive achievements related to proper ethics.

Superiority of Ethics on the Second Ground Over the First Ground

QUESTION: Does a first ground Bodhisattva not accumulate all ten of these paths of actions?

ANSWER: Chandrakirti's root text says:

19ab   *For him these ten paths of virtue,*
    Perfected, are extremely pure.

A first grounder does accumulate all these, but for a second grounder these ten paths of virtuous actions are perfected and become extremely pure. This does not occur for a first grounder.

The teaching that giving is surpassing on the first ground indicates that Bodhisattvas remain in possession of it on the higher ground. It is said that ethics is surpassing on the second ground because from among the nine remaining perfections a Bodhisattva does not have the measure of perfect practice – which he has with respect to ethics – in relation to patience and so forth. Thus, this does not mean that he does not have the remaining perfections.

The ten virtues are mentioned to illustrate the formulations of ethics based on them, and the Bodhisattva maintains all those of proper ethics.

Chandrakirti's root text says:

19cd   *Like an autumn moon he is always pure,*
    Beautified by them, serene and radiant.

One whose ethics are so pure is like an autumn moon that extinguishes the pain of heat and abides glittering with white light. Just so, one always abiding in pure ethics has the serenity of having restrained the doors of the senses and has the radiance of a glitteringly clear body, and thus he is beautified by his ethics.

Another Cause of the Thorough Purification of Ethics
Chandrakirti's root text says:

20ab   *If he views his ethics as inherently pure,*
       Then their purity will not be complete.

Some monks engage in very pure ethics based on [vows of] individual emancipation. However, if they do not abandon the view that phenomena inherently exist, then their ethics will not be pure but will be faulty though apparently proper. The *Pile of Jewels Sutra* says:

> Kashyapa, some monks have proper ethics; they abide restrained by vows of individual emancipation. Their rites and spheres of activity are perfect, and they view even coarse and subtle transgressions with concern. They thoroughly assume and train in the precepts and possess pure activities of body, speech, and mind. Hence their livelihood is thoroughly pure, but they propound a self. Kashyapa, they are the first of those seeming to have proper ethics which in fact are faulty . . . .Furthermore, Kashyapa, even though some monks thoroughly assume the twelve qualities of training, they view them with apprehension [of inherent existence]. Abiding in the conceptions of 'I' and 'mine', Kashyapa, they are the fourth of those whose ethics appear to be proper but are faulty.

'Propound a self' means viewing with apprehension [of inherent existence]. This is indicated by the fact that they abide in the conceptions of 'I' and 'mine', the meaning of which should not be understood as referring to the common false view of the transitory collection but as not having abandoned the [subtle] conception that 'I' and 'mine' exist by way of their own nature.

The word 'he' in the first line of stanza twenty cannot refer to the Bodhisattva mentioned in stanza nineteen; therefore, Nak-tso translated these two lines this way:

> If he viewed his ethics as inherently pure
> Then his ethics would be faulty.

His translation as 'then' [the hypothetical] is good [since a Bodhisattva Superior would never make this error].

Chandrakirti's root text says:

20cd   *Thus he always forsakes completely the wandering*
         Of the dualistic intellect toward the three.

If the view apprehending [inherent existence] is not abandoned, ethics are not pure. Thus, a second grounder always completely forsakes, or frees himself from, the wanderings of the dualistic intellect that views as inherently existent dualistic phenomena such as things and non-things. Here the view of inherent existence is forsaken with respect to the three – the sentient being with respect to whom faulty ethics are abandoned, the antidote used to abandon them, and the agent of abandonment.

PRAISE OF ETHICS

This section has five parts, enjoying the fruits of giving in a happy migration depends on ethics, enjoying the fruits of giving in continuous lives depends on ethics, liberation from bad migrations is extremely difficult for one bereft of ethics, reason for discoursing on ethics after discoursing on giving, and praising ethics as a cause of both high status and definite goodness.

Enjoying the Fruits of Giving in a Happy Migration Depends on Ethics

Having said that the Bodhisattva's ethics are perfect, Chandrakirti shows that although in general those of others [such as Hearers] can be perfect, the features of a Bodhisattva's ethics are far greater than those of giving and so forth and serve as the base of all marvellous qualities. His root text says:

21ab   *The arising in bad migrations of resources from giving*
         Is due to a being's losing his legs of ethics.

From gifts given by donors with good ethics, special marvellous resources will arise during their lives as gods and humans. The arising of various marvellous resources in a birth in a bad migration, such as a being in a trifling hell or an ox, horse, elephant, monkey, dragon, or a hungry ghost with great magical powers, is due to that being's having lost or been separated from his legs of ethics [that would have taken him to a good migration].

This indicates that if you lack proper ethics, the resources that are the fruit of giving will mature not in a happy migration but in a bad one. Since maturation of the effects of giving on the base of a happy migration is needed, a donor of gifts as explained above should – if he wants a happy migration – keep proper ethics.

Enjoying the Fruits of Giving in Continuous Lives Depends on Ethics

If one lacks ethics, the fruits of giving ripen on the base of a bad migration. Merely enjoying the fruits of former giving on that base, one gives nothing newly due to extreme stupidity. Chandrakirti's root text says:

21cd *Having spent completely both principal and interest*
   He will be without resources in the future.

Since the principal as well as the interest is used, it is completely consumed. Once the fruits of former giving have been spent, that person will be without resources.

For instance, someone who has gained much produce from planting a few seeds plants even more for the sake of increase, due to which his great stores are not exhausted. However, a fool merely enjoys his harvest instead of planting more seeds and thus does not continuously increase it.

Liberation from Bad Migrations is Extremely Difficult for One Bereft of Ethics

It is extremely difficult for one whose legs of ethics are broken to attain continual increase of resources. Moreover this leads to bad migrations from which it is very hard to escape. Chandrakirti's root text says:

22 *If when acting freely and living agreeably,*
  He does not act to hold [himself back from falling down],
  He will fall into an abyss and lose control;
  How will he raise himself from there in the future?

A person who abides in a divine or human migration acts freely according to his own wish. He does not depend on others, but like a hero free from bondage abides in an agreeable land. If he does not act to hold himself from falling into a bad migration, he will be like a hero bound and cast into a great ravine. Having fallen into the chasm of a bad migration, he will have no independence and will lose control. By what means will he raise himself from that state in the future? He cannot.

It is extremely rare to achieve virtue during a bad migration, in which the accumulation of sins is extremely powerful; thus, one must continue in only bad migrations. A sutra says, 'Even if one is born among humans, this is an achievement of two maturations.' Thus, it is said that birth as a human is difficult [to attain].

Therefore, from now on you must keep yourself from falling into a bad migration. You should know that this means striving at proper ethics.

Reason for Discoursing on Ethics after Discoursing on Giving
Chandrakirti's root text says:

23 *Thus the Conqueror, having discoursed on giving,*
  Spoke upon its accompaniment by ethics.
  When virtues are nurtured on the field of ethics,
  The enjoyment of effects is unceasing.

Faulty ethics is a source of many faults, such as being led to a bad migration; therefore, immediately after discoursing on giving, the Conqueror who had overcome all sins spoke on the achievement of accompanying giving with ethics so that the benefits thereof would not be wasted. The reason for this is that ethics is the base of all auspicious qualities and, therefore, is alone the field. If the virtues of giving and so forth are nurtured on the field of ethics, the continuation of engaging in causes, such as giving, and of using effects, such as a good body and good resources, will increase more and more. The collections of effects grow, and one is able to enjoy them for a long time. Otherwise, this is a not possible.

This indicates that givers of gifts should not just consider the marvellous resources that are effects of giving but should think about the physical support with which they will enjoy them. They should consider the continuation of resources in many lives. Thus, you should know that keeping proper ethics – the means of achieving these – is very important.

Novice Bodhisattvas should, as was explained before, make effort at giving gifts, and they should do this in order to attain Buddhahood for the sake of all sentient beings, who are their field of intent. Temporarily, however, they need a ripening of fruits of giving on the base of a happy migration over many lifetimes. This too depends on ethics because without them the favourable circumstances for training in the Bodhisattva deeds are not complete.

Praising Ethics as a Cause of Both High Status and Definite Goodness

Both the body of a happy migrator and the enjoyment on that base of the fruits of giving for a long time depend on ethics, which are also necessary for the achievement of definite goodness [liberation from cyclic existence and omniscience]. Chandrakirti's root text says:

24 *For common beings, those born from the word,*
   Those set toward solitary enlightenment, and
   Conqueror Children, a cause of definite goodness
   And high status is none other than proper ethics.

None other than ethics is a cause of high status for common beings who have not entered the path and a cause of definite goodness – enlightenment – for Hearers born from the Subduer's word and those set on the path of a Solitary Realizer's enlightenment as well as for Conqueror Chidren – Bodhisattvas.

There are, however, many other causes which are not ethics. Thus, this means that in order to achieve special high status and definite goodness a definite relation with ethics is necessary. If ethics are forsaken, there is no way that these can be accomplished.

This has been a summary of meanings set forth in the *Sutra on the Ten Grounds*. There it is explained:

> Each of the ten non-virtues – killing and so forth – are divided into great, middling, and small which lead respectively to [migrations as] a hell-being, animal, and hungry ghost. Finally, if one is born among humans, killing causes a short life and many diseases. Each of the remaining nine non-virtues also produces two undesirables [a birth in a bad migration and later birth as an unfortunate human]. The ten virtues cause birth as a desire god, a human, [and a being in any of the higher realms] up through the Peak of Cyclic Existence.
>
> Higher than that is practice of the ten virtues in conjunction with a trifling attitude aimed at one's own welfare alone together with renunciation and fear of cyclic existence. When the ten virtues are practised with this aspect lacking great compassion yet having the wisdom cognizing selflessness that is induced by others' words, then one comes to be liberated through the Hearer Vehicle.
>
> Still higher is the practice of one who in his final cyclic existence does not depend on others and aims at the enlightenment of a Solitary Realizer. If one practises thus without great compassion and skill in means but penetrates the suchness of profound dependent-arising, one is definitely freed through the Solitary Realizer Vehicle.
>
> Above that is the practice of one with extremely vast and immeasurable mercy, compassion, and skill in means. If one practises thus, establishing great waves of prayer petitions, not casting aside any sentient being, but aiming at the extremely vast Buddha wisdom, one is thoroughly purified through the mind of enlightenment and accomplishes the vast deeds of the pure perfections.

Nagarjuna says in his *Friendly Letter* that training in proper ethics is very important:

You should observe ethics that are not low,
Not degenerate, not mixed, and not polluted.
Ethics are said to be the base of all attainments
As is the earth for all that does and does not move.

Therefore, although ethics is set forth in connection with the second ground, novice Bodhisattvas should also practise them. They should think about the great importance of ethics, restraining their minds without being moved by tendencies toward the ten non-virtues. As Chandrakirti says (24):

> For common beings, those born from the word,
> Those set toward solitary enlightenment, and
> Conqueror Children, a cause of definite goodness
> And high status is none other than proper ethics.

Then, they should train in conjoining the practice of proper ethics with the wisdom that cognizes the unapprehendability [of inherent existence]. Since merely understanding or familiarizing with these only a few times brings nothing, these meanings should be contemplated continuously. If they familiarize with them continuously, they will spontaneously engage in the modes of training of the Bodhisattva deeds – even those that generate mental discomfort when first heard and those that our Teacher [Buddha] could not practise for a long time. Ratnadasa's *Praise of Endless Qualities (Guṇaparyantastotra)* says:

> Those deeds, which when heard of harm the worldly
> And which you could not practise for a long time,
> Will in time become spontaneous for all familiar with them.
> Ones not so familiar find it hard to increase attainments.

EXAMPLE OF NON-MIXTURE WITH WHAT IS NOT
CONDUCIVE TO ETHICS

Chandrakirti's root text says:

> 25 *Just as an ocean is incompatible with a corpse*
> *And just as prosperity is incompatible with calamity,*
> *So a great being subdued by ethics*
> *Does not wish to live with faulty ethics.*

For instance, a great ocean – due to the power of the cleanly dragons abiding there – does not dwell compatibly with a corpse but with its waves pushes it to the shore. Also, the marvels of prosperity and the bad fortunes of calamity are incompatible. Similarly, a second grounder, a great being subdued by pure ethics, does not wish to live with faulty ethics.

Chandrakirti's commentary on Aryadeva's *Four Hundred* says, 'Calamity definitely exists in a household where Lucky resides.' However, this does not contradict his explanation here because in his commentary to the *Four Hundred* he was thinking of two persons having those names whereas here in the *Supplement* 'calamity' means misfortune.

DIVISIONS OF THE PERFECTION OF ETHICS

Chandrakirti's root text says:

26 *If there be any apprehension of the three –*
    Forsaken by whom, what, and with regard to whom –
    Such ethics are described as being a mundane perfection.
    That empty of attachment to the three is supramundane.

If one is unable to put an end to the seeds of apprehending the true existence of the three spheres – the object of abandonment which is being forsaken, the person by whom it is forsaken, and the sentient being with regard to whom it is being forsaken – then such ethics are described as a mundane perfection. If ethics are conjoined with the uncontaminated wisdom realizing unapprehendability – that is to say, are empty of attachment apprehending true existence in the three spheres as explained above – then they are supramundane. Thus, ethics have two divisions [mundane and supramundane].

CONCLUSION BY WAY OF EXPRESSING THE
FEATURES OF THE SECOND GROUND

Chandrakirti's root text says:

27 *Like the light of an autumn moon, the Stainless*
    Arising from the moon of a Conqueror Child,

Though not worldly, the glory of the world,
Removes the mental distress of migrators.

Just as stainless autumn moonlight relieves creatures from the discomforts [caused by heat], so the second ground, the Stainless, removes the distress of migrators generated by faulty ethics. The Stainless arises from the moon of a Conqueror Child who is a second grounder and is so called because it has the light of pure ethics free from the stains of the faulty.

Because a second grounder is not included among those who wander in cyclic existence, he is not mundane – not of cyclic existence – but he is the glory of the world. This is because all marvellous attainments flow from this Bodhisattva, and he, through the power of prayer petitions for the sake of sentient beings, has attained the sublime cause of universal monarchy over the four continents.

Such is the explanation of the second ultimate mind generation in the *Illumination of the Thought, An Extensive Explanation of Chandrakirti's 'Supplement to the Middle Way'*.

11 Perfection of Patience

THIRD GROUND, THE LUMINOUS

This section has four parts, (1) describing the ground – the base of qualities, (2) qualifying features of the ground, (3) distinguishing attribute of the first three perfections, and (4) conclusion by way of expressing the features of the third ground.

DESCRIPTION OF THE THIRD GROUND – THE BASE OF QUALITIES

Chandrakirti's root text says:

28   *Because the light of the fire wholly consuming*
      The fuel of objects of knowledge arises,
      This third ground is called the Luminous, for a copper
      Splendour like the sun appears to the Sugata Child.

The third Bodhisattva ground is called the Luminous. Why is it so named? It accords with the meaning of its name because when the third ground is attained, the fire of wisdom burning all the fuel of objects of knowledge arises along with a light which by nature is able to extinguish all elaborations of duality during meditative equipoise. Furthermore, just as a copper-like splendour appears shortly before sunrise, so on this ground an illumination of wisdom appears to a Bodhisattva, a Sugata Child who has generated the third ground. This indicates that on the third ground an appearance of all-pervasive red or orange light appears subsequent to meditative equipoise.

Nagarjuna's *Precious Garland* (444–6) says:

The third ground is called the Luminous because
The pacifying light of wisdom appears.
The concentrations and clairvoyances are generated
While desire and hatred are extinguished completely.

Through the maturation of these qualities
He practises supremely the deeds of patience
And putting an end to desire completely
Becomes a great wise king of the gods.

QUALIFYING FEATURES OF THE THIRD GROUND

This section has four parts, surpassing patience on the third ground, way of observing other patience, divisions of the perfection of patience, and other pure features arising on the third ground.

Surpassing Patience on the Third Ground

In order to indicate that a Bodhisattva who has found such illumination of wisdom has a surpassing perfection of patience, Chandrakirti says in his root text:

29   *Though another, unjustifiably disturbed*
       By anger, cuts from his body flesh and bone
       Bit by bit for a long time, he generates
       Patience strongly toward the mutilator.

Since surpassing giving and ethics, which were explained earlier, are possessed on this higher ground, here from among the remaining eight perfections patience is surpassing. It is surpassing in that the measure of advancement in the practice of this perfection is not present in the remaining seven.

A third ground Bodhisattva protects the minds of others and possesses the peace of wisdom as explained in the previous stanza. Thus, though others might generate qualms that serve as a basis of harmful intent by thinking, 'In the past he harmed me and my friends,' 'He harms us now,' or 'He will harm us in the future,' he does not engage in such activities of body, speech, and mind. Therefore, Chandrakirti qualifies the Bodhisattva as an unjustified source of anger.

Even if someone, disturbed by such anger, cuts from the body of this Bodhisattva not just flesh but also bone, not in large sections but bit by bit, not continually but pausing in between, and not finishing in a short time but cutting over a long period, the Bodhisattva would not get angry at the mutilator. Instead, he would generate very strong patience by taking cognizance of the mutilator and realizing that due to this sin this person will experience suffering as a hell-being and so forth even greater than that of other hell-beings.

This is what it means to have surpassing patience. Therefore, it is clear that such patience is not generated on the Very Joyful or the Stainless Grounds even though a first or second ground Bodhisattva's mental continuum is not disturbed when his body is cut. Hence, it should be understood that surpassing patience first arises on the third ground.

Chandrakirti's root text says:

> 30 *Also through viewing these phenomena*
> *As like reflections – what Bodhisattva*
> *Seeing selflessness is cut, by whom,*
> *Just how, and when – he will be patient.*

Not only does a third ground Bodhisattva have surpassing patience that observes the great suffering of hell-beings and so forth, he also sees clearly the phenomena of the three spheres as like reflections. Because the three – by whom the body of a Bodhisattva seeing selflessness is cut, what is cut, in what manner and at what time – are vividly seen in this way and because he does not discriminate falsely about 'I' and 'mine', the Bodhisattva will be patient.

Chandrakirti's commentary[92] explains that the word 'also' [in the first line] of the stanza is 'for the sake of including the causes of patience'. Thus, his patience results from this cause as well as the former causes of non-disturbance which were just explained. Furthermore, Chandrakirti[93] says, 'Because of this also', and thus the verse should be translated as 'also through viewing' [instead of 'because of viewing', as it was in Tibetan].

Way of Observing Other Patience

This section has two parts, unsuitability of anger and suitability of observing patience.

Unsuitability of Anger

This section has four parts, unsuitability of anger due to its being senseless and very faulty, contradiction of not wanting suffering in the future and making harmful response, unsuitability of anger due to its destroying virtue accumulated over a long time, and stopping anger by reflecting on the many faults of impatience.

Unsuitability of Anger due to Its Being Senseless and Very Faulty

Patience is not just a practice suited to the minds of those on Bodhisattva paths, for it causes those not abiding on a ground to maintain all attainments without diminishment. Therefore, it is fitting for those lacking patience to avoid anger. Chandrakirti's root text says:

31 *If you get angry with someone who has done you harm,*
    Is that harm stopped because of your resentment of him?
    Resentment thus is certainly senseless here
    And unfavourable for future lives.

If you become angry at someone who harmed you, then since the harm cannot be reversed, does resenting him reverse the harm already done? It does not. Therefore, resentment is certainly senseless here.

Resentment is an irritable coarse disposition, synonymous with belligerence. Not only is it purposeless, but it is also unfavourable to your welfare in future lives because time spent in anger impels unpleasant fruition after death.

Contradiction of Not Wanting Suffering in the Future and Making Harmful Response

Some people, when suffering due to former bad deeds, are

influenced by their obscuration to think, 'Another has harmed me,' and generate anger toward the harmer. They want to prevent the arising of the suffering that involves such harm in the future by making a harmful response. In order to overcome this [tendency] Chandrakirti says in his root text:

32   *How could it be right for one, wishing to assert that*
      He is finishing the effects of non-virtuous
      Actions done earlier, to sow the seeds of
      Suffering through harming and hating others?

The great suffering that enemies inflict on one's body is an effect of the non-virtuous action of killing one did in the past. That effect can be experienced as a strong fruition in the three bad migrations. Also, those for whom effects still remain [after a lifetime in a bad migration] undergo unpleasantness by way of fruits similar to that cause [upon rebirth as a human]. How could it be right for one, who wishes to say that he is finishing the remaining effects of those actions in order to overcome such unpleasantness, to sow the seeds or causes of future suffering? That suffering will be far greater than he is experiencing here, and he is led to it through making harmful answers to others and disturbing his continuum from within through anger. It is not suitable.

Therefore, just as one bears the pain of bloodletting with a sharp instrument as a physician's means of healing disease, it is very suitable to bear small superficial suffering for the sake of overcoming limitless deep suffering.

Unsuitability of Anger due to its Destroying Virtue Accumulated over a Long Time

This section has two parts, meaning of the text and ancillary meanings.

Meaning of the Text on the Unsuitability of Anger due to its Destroying Virtue Accumulated over a Long Time

Impatience not only is a cause projecting vast unpleasantness as its fruition but also consumes collections of merit accumu-

lated over a long time. Indicating this, Chandrakirti's root text
says:

33 *One moment of hating a Conqueror Child destroys*
The virtues arising from giving and ethics
Accumulated for a hundred aeons.
Thus there can be no [worse] sin than impatience.

When a Bodhisattva, a great being, generates an angry thought
toward a Conqueror Child, who already has an altruistic mind
of enlightenment, he does so through forcefully imputing true
and untrue faults. Either he does not determine that the person
is a Bodhisattva or, despite so determining, he is influenced by
his strong habituation to the afflictions. Even if a Bodhisattva
generates anger toward another Bodhisattva for just a moment,
accumulations of merit amassed over a hundred aeons – virtues
arising from the perfections of giving and ethics which were
explained before – are destroyed. If that is the case, then what
need is there to say anything about one who is not a Bodhisattva
getting angry with one who is?

Just as one cannot measure the amount of water in a great
ocean, so one cannot ascertain the limits [of suffering] that
results from being angry with a Bodhisattva. In terms of projecting unpleasant effects and harming virtue there is no
greater sin than impatient anger.

[Jaya-ananda] says in his *Explanation* that 'imputing true
faults' refers to falsely imputing bigness to small [faults].

With respect to Chandrakirti's explanation that roots of
virtue are destroyed by anger, the *Manjushri Sport Sutra*
(*Mañjushrīvikrīḍita*) says, 'Manjushri, anger destroys virtue
accumulated over a hundred aeons.' It is not clear in that sutra
whether the object of anger and the base of anger [the person
who is angered] are Bodhisattvas or not; however, in his commentary Chandrakirti[94] explains it within the context of both
the object and the base being Bodhisattvas.

Prior to quoting this sutra, Nagarjuna quotes the *Lion's
Roar of Maitreya Sutra* (*Maitreyamahāsimhanāda*) in his *Compendium of Sutra*:

Merely by attacking all sentient beings in the realms of a thousand world systems having a billion worlds with reproach, rebuke, sticks, and fists, a Bodhisattva does not wound or scar himself. However, he is wounded and scarred even by generating harmful intent, obstinacy, or a mind of hatred for another Bodhisattva. Why? Even if he does not lose [the path of] omniscience completely, the Bodhisattva must from that time wear the armour [practise the six perfections] for as many aeons as there were thoughts of harm, obstinacy, and hatred generated toward the other Bodhisattva.

Thus it is clear that Chandrakirti bases his commentary on this rendition in which both the object and the base of anger are Bodhisattvas. [The reference in the *Lion's Roar of Maitreya* is to a lesser unprophesied Bodhisattva's being angry with a prophesied Bodhisattva.][95]

QUESTION: Why do the masters Shura [Ashvaghosha] and Shantideva say that the virtue accumulated over a thousand aeons is destroyed? Shantideva's *Engaging in the Bodhisattva Deeds* (VI.1) says:

> One moment's hatred destroys
> All the good deeds of giving,
> Worshipping Sugatas, and so forth
> Amassed over a thousand aeons.

ANSWER: Although Prajnakaramati's commentary on Shantideva's *Engaging in the Bodhisattva Deeds* says that being angry with sentient beings destroys the virtue accumulated over many thousands of aeons, it is difficult to believe. The two masters [Ashvaghosha and Shantideva] do not clearly identify the object and the base; however, only a Bodhisattva is an object of anger that destroys roots of virtue accumulated over a hundred or a thousand aeons.

If on the basis of the reference to 'a Bodhisattva, a great being' (p. 209) we make an inference about the base of anger in [Chandrakirti's text], it appears that he is a Bodhisattva of greater power than the Bodhisattva who is the object. Furthermore, [in general] the base of anger is definitely a Bodhisattva who is a common being [on the paths of accumulation and preparation], but the object can be either a Bodhisattva who has attained a ground or who has not. Thus, there are three hatreds – by a Bodhisattva of greater power to a lesser, by a lesser to a greater, and by one to another equal in power. When a Bodhisattva of greater power becomes angry at one of lesser power, virtue accumulated over a hundred aeons is destroyed, and when one who is not a Bodhisattva is angry with one who is, it is clear that virtue accumulated over a thousand aeons is destroyed.

I will analyse in relation to scripture the destruction of virtuous roots when a lesser Bodhisattva becomes angry with a greater one and when a Bodhisattva is angry with an equal. I will also analyse the destruction of roots of virtue in relation to the status of the object when a lesser becomes angry with a greater.

[Lesser Bodhisattva Being Angry with a Greater]

The first part of the quote from the *Lion's Roar of Maitreya Sutra* – 'Merely by attacking all sentient beings in the realms of a thousand world systems having a billion worlds with reproach, rebuke, sticks, and fists, a Bodhisattva does not wound or scar himself' – sets forth an instance of a Bodhisattva's being angry with non-Bodhisattvas, abusing them with speech and striking them physically. This is shown to differ from wounding or scarring a Bodhisattva; hence, it should be known that it is not necessary for a Bodhisattva who becomes angry with one who is not to bear the armour from the very beginning. It is indicated that if a Bodhisattva merely generates an angry thought toward a Bodhisattva without any physical or verbal expression, he must bear the armour from the beginning for as many aeons as the times that he generated the thought. The object of such is clearly a Bodhisattva who has been prophesied, and the base is clearly one who has not. The *Condensed Perfection of Wisdom Sutra (Sañchayagāthāprajñāpāramitā)* says:

If a Bodhisattva who has not been prophesied
Angers and disputes with another who has so been,
He must bear the armour from the beginning for as many
Aeons as the times his mind was imbued with hatred.

With respect to the necessity of bearing the armour from the
beginning, if, for example, one who has the capacity to pass
quickly from a Bodhisattva's great path of accumulation to a
path of preparation becomes angry at another who has been
prophesied, he cannot pass to the path of preparation for as
many aeons as the number of instants of anger and must train
in the path from the beginning.

[*A Bodhisattva Being Angry with an Equal*]

Shantideva's *Engaging in the Bodhisattva Deeds* (I. 34) says:

The Subduer said that one who generates
A bad mind to such a Conqueror Child patron[96]
Will stay in a hell for as many aeons as there were
Instants of the bad mind which he generated.

Thus, it is said that one will abide in a hell for as many aeons
as there were instants of developing hatred for a Bodhisattva.
There is also the fault of destroying roots of virtue accumulated
over many aeons.

If a non-prophesied Bodhisattva is angry with a prophesied
one, his detention in a hell is similar to that just explained, and
he must also bear the armour from the beginning for as many
aeons. The *Compendium of All the Weaving Sutra* (*Sarvavaid-alyasaṃgraha*) says that if one abandons the doctrine as set forth
in the sutra but confesses the fault three times daily for seven
years, the fruition of that deed is purified, but even at the fastest
ten aeons are necessary to attain endurance [facility allowing
progress to the next path]. Thus, even though confession and
restraint in many ways does not restore a path that has become
slower, it will purify experience of the fruition. Hence, you
should make effort at confession and restraint.

Ancillary Meanings

When anger is generated, it destroys roots of virtue even if neither the object nor the base are Bodhisattvas. Shantideva quotes a Sarvastivada scripture [the *Questions of Upali Sutra* (Upāliparipṛchchhā)] in his *Compendium of Instructions:*

'Monks, a monk pays homage with all his limbs to a reliquary of hair or nails; he makes his mind pure and thus is holy. Monks, this monk will enjoy the reign of a universal monarch for a thousand times the number of grains of sand beneath him extending 84,000 yojanas to the sphere of gold' . . . Then the distinguished Upali paid homage by joining his palms in the direction of the Blessed One and asked him, 'Since the Blessed One has said that the virtuous roots of monks are so great, then, O Blessed One, in what situation are virtuous roots diminished, thoroughly reduced, and completely extinguished?' 'Upali, I do not see such wounding and scarring [from other non-virtues], but when one whose behaviour is pure generates a bad intention toward one having pure behaviour,[97] Upali, through that these great roots of virtue are diminished, thoroughly reduced, and completely consumed. Therefore, Upali, if it is unsuitable to mentally harm even sticks, what need is there to mention a conscious body?'

'Diminish' refers to lessening the increase of very great and marvellous roots of virtue and shortening those of long increase; not destroying all the effects, it is a small extinguishment. 'Reduction' is a middling extinguishment [leaving no more than a little fruition], and 'complete consumption' is a great one [entirely destroying the possibility of fruition].[98]

The *Moon Lamp Sutra* (*Chandrapradīpa, Samādhirāja*) quoted in Nagarjuna's *Compendium of Sutra* says:

For one who thinks to harm his companions
Proper ethics and hearing will not protect him,
Neither will concentration and retreat,
Nor giving and worshiping the Buddhas.

'Companions' are those engaging in pure behaviour. Non-protection by the six – ethics and so forth – means that these cannot stop the destruction of roots of virtue by anger. The earlier parts of that sutra do not explain clearly which roots of virtue are destroyed, but Shantideva's *Engaging in the Bodhisattva Deeds* explains them as, 'Giving, worshiping Sugatas, and so forth,' and Chandrakirti's *Supplement* [stanza 33] explains them as having arisen from giving and ethics; his commentary[99] explains them as 'the collections of merit'. Therefore, it seems that this does not apply to the virtuous roots of having cognized selflessness well, but this is to be analysed.

OBJECTION: The *Teaching of Akshayamati Sutra* (*Akshayamatinirdesha*), as quoted in Nagarjuna's *Compendium of Sutra*, gives the example of a drop of water that has fallen into a great ocean and has not been consumed for a great aeon. The sutra says that a virtuous root dedicated to enlightenment will not be consumed until enlightenment. The *Array of Stalks Sutra* (*Gaṇḍavyūha*) also takes as an example an ounce of a type of quicksilver called 'gold-appearing' which although it transforms a thousand ounces of iron into gold cannot be dissipated by that iron. The sutra says that the element of quicksilver of an altruistic mind generation to enlightenment cannot be consumed by all the iron of contaminated actions and afflictions. Thus, is it not that altruistic mind generation, virtues conjoined with it, and virtues dedicated to enlightenment cannot be destroyed by anger?

ANSWER: It is not so because the destruction of virtuous roots in Bodhisattvas who are great beings is also mentioned. The meaning of the former passage [in the *Teaching of Akshayamati*] is that virtuous roots are not consumed through the emergence of their effects; however, it is not that anger does not consume them. The meaning of the second passage [in the *Array of Stalks*] is that contaminated actions and afflictions cannot waste an altruistic mind generation in the way that contaminated actions and afflictions can be wasted in dependence on altruistic mind generation.

Some explain the meaning of destroying virtuous roots this way:[100] 'The capacity of former virtues to generate their effects quickly is overcome, and the emergence of effects is postponed. [In the meantime] the effects of former hatred, for instance, emerge, but it is not that the effects of the virtues will not emerge when the proper circumstances are eventually encountered. Since no worldly path can abandon seeds to be abandoned, afflictions could not abandon [virtuous] seeds.'

ANSWER: That is inconclusive because although the virtue of a common being's purification of non-virtue through the power of the four antidotes[101] does not abandon the seeds [of non-virtue], a fruition [of the non-virtues purified] will never emerge even though the proper circumstances are encountered. Also, at the time of attaining the levels of peak and forbearance on the path of preparation, one has not abandoned non-virtuous seeds that would cause wrong views or bad migrations; however, even if the proper circumstances are encountered, one never generates wrong views or takes rebirth in a bad migration.

Furthermore, a sutra quoted in Vasubandhu's commentary to his *Treasury of Knowledge* says:

Actions cause fruition
In cyclic existence – first the heavy,
Then the proximate, then the accustomed,
Then what was done before.

Thus, through the prior fruition of a virtuous or non-virtuous action, the opportunity for fruition of other actions is temporarily blocked; however, one cannot posit that a virtue or non-virtue has been overcome merely because of this, and no such claim has been made. If this were the case, one would have to say that all powerful non-virtuous actions overpower virtuous roots. Bhavaviveka's commentary on his *Essence of the Middle Way* [the *Blaze of Reasoning* (*Tarkajvālā*)] says that just as a shoot will not be produced from a ruined seed even in the proper conditions, so when a non-virtue is purified by the four powers or when a virtuous root is overcome through wrong views or harmful intent, their effects cannot emerge even when the proper circumstances are eventually encountered.

Also, the overcoming of a virtue does not mean that a virtue in one's continuum ceases to exist after one generates anger; rather, anger harms the virtue's capacity to issue forth an effect. The extent to which later fruition is harmed accords with the amount of harm done, causing a small, middling, or great extinguishment of virtue as explained above.

Thus, harm is incurred in two ways: the capacity to generate a new path quickly is overcome and the generation of effects such as happy migrations is undermined. Nagarjuna's *Compendium of Sutra* sets forth the limitless fault of hating, despising, and criticizing Bodhisattvas with bad motivation. Ascertaining or not ascertaining that a person is a Bodhisattva and having true or untrue reasons for anger are said to be similar. Therefore, you should strive as hard as you can to stop anger in general and in particular that aimed at Bodhisattvas and those whose behaviour is pure.

The *Akashagarbha Sutra* (*Ākāshagarbha*) says that root infractions [of Bodhisattva vows] destroy roots of virtue previously generated. Also, Shantideva's *Compendium of Instructions* states that aspiring to a household because of strong attachment to goods, being inflated with the pride of conceit [boasting that one has attainments not yet acquired],[102] and forsaking the doctrine are acts that destroy virtues formerly generated and deprive one of progress based on virtuous practice. Therefore, having identified the conditions for destroying virtuous roots, you should forsake them with strong force.

This is just a brief account. You definitely should look at Nagarjuna's *Compendium of Sutra* and Shantideva's *Compendium of Instructions*.

Stopping Anger by Reflecting on the Many Faults of Impatience

Chandrakirti's root text says:

34abc It creates an ugly form, leads to the unholy,
   And robs discrimination that knows right and wrong.
   Through impatience one is quickly cast into a bad migration.

Impatience in one who is powerless destroys only himself, but impatience in the powerful and non-compassionate destroys both self and others. Merely generating it, one's face becomes ugly, one is led to the unholy and robbed of the discrimination that thinks, 'This is a right and that is a wrong way to act.' Through impatience – anger – one is quickly cast into a bad migration after death.

Having reflected on these faults, do whatever you can to stop anger through thinking that there is no occasion for it.

Suitability of Observing Patience

This section has two parts, reflecting on the many advantages of patience and a summary exhortation to observe patience.

Reflecting on the Many Advantages of Patience

QUESTION: If those are the disadvantages of impatience, what are the advantages of its opposite, patience?

ANSWER: Chandrakirti's root text says:

34d–35   *Patience creates qualities opposite to those*
      Explained above. Through patience comes beauty, dearness
      To the holy, skill in discriminating between
      The right and wrong, birth afterwards as a human
      Or god, and the extinguishment of non-virtues.

Through cultivating patience, qualities opposite to the faults of impatience explained above are created. One attains a beautiful body, is dear to and cherished by holy beings, becomes skilled in knowing the right – the suitable – and the wrong – the unsuitable, after death takes birth as a human or god, and removes non-virtues accumulated through anger and so forth.

Reflecting on these, you should generate the power of patience.

Summary Exhortation to Observe Patience

Chandrakirti's root text says:

36 *Ordinary beings and Conqueror Children,*
    Realizing the faults of anger and advantages of patience
    And forsaking impatience, should quickly and always observe
    The patience praised by Superior Beings.

One should realize, as explained above, the disadvantageous faults of common beings' anger and the beneficial advantages of Conqueror Children's patience. Having forsaken impatience, one should always observe the patience praised by Superior Beings.

Divisions of the Perfection of Patience

In his basic text Chandrakirti indicates that the perfection of patience has two divisions, mundane and supramundane:

37 *Though dedicated to enlightenment of perfect Buddhahood,*
    [Patience] is mundane if one apprehends the three.
    [Patience] that does not involve such apprehension
    Buddha taught as a perfection supramundane.

This can be understood from the former explanations [of the perfections of giving and ethics pages 188–90 and 220].

Other Pure Features Arising on the Third Ground

Chandrakirti's root text says:

38 *On this ground the Conqueror Child has the concentrations*
    And clairvoyances. Desire and hatred are extinguished.
    Always he is able to overcome
    The world's lustful desires as well.

Just as on the third ground a Conqueror Child has the pure perfection of patience, so he attains the four pure concentrations. This implies that he also attains the four pure formless absorptions – limitless space, limitless consciousness, nothingness, and the peak of cyclic existence – as well as the four pure immeasurables – love, compassion, joy, and equanimity – and the five pure clairvoyances – magical creations, the divine ear, knowing others' minds, remembering former lives, and the divine eye.

Though he enters into and rises from the concentrations and

formless absorptions, he is intent on seeing the thorough completion of the causes of enlightenment. Thus, he is born by the power of prayer petitions and not by that of these worldly concentrations and formless absorptions. Though he did indeed attain these on the first ground, here he attains a training in higher meditative stabilization far superior to what he had on the preceding grounds. Since there are [now] greater doubts about whether he might be reborn by the power of these concentrations and absorptions, it is discussed here [in connection with the third ground].

On this ground an extinguishment of desire and hatred is attained. The word 'and' [in the second line of stanza 38] means 'also' and includes an unmentioned extinguishment of ignorance. This 'extinguishment' is not complete because the *Sutra on the Ten Grounds* says that all the four fetters – desire, form [attachment to the form realm], existence [attachment to the formless realm], and ignorance – are *diminished* [not completely destroyed].

According to Asanga's *Bodhisattva Level* (*Bodhisattvabhūmi*) the meaning of these is that through the power of meditative stabilization in the worldly concentrations and formless absorptions one becomes free from attachment to [the realms of] desire, form, and formlessness – this being an abandonment of the manifest as explained before. Therefore, the sutra distinctly says 'diminished'. Also, the fetters are clearly those explained in the *Knowledges* [and not the uncommon afflictions as explained in the Prasangika system].

On this, the *Sutra on the Ten Grounds* [quoted in Chandrakirti's commentary][103] says, 'The fetters which are views were abandoned earlier.' Some explain this as meaning that the latter three views [perverse view, conceiving bad ethics as well as codes of behaviour as superior, and conceiving bad views as superior] were abandoned on the path of seeing, but it should be taken as referring to having abandoned [all] five artificial views on the first ground [including that of the transitory collection as real 'I' and 'mine' and views holding to extremes]. Asanga's *Bodhisattva Level* says, 'The fetters which are views were abandoned [in manifest form] first from the level of engagement through belief [on the paths of accumulation and preparation] by believing in the suchness that is the nature of phenomena.' Further on, the sutra says that wrong desire, hatred, and ignorance which had not decreased over a hundred trillion aeons are abandoned on the third ground. This refers to abandoning the seeds, which in turn refers to the objects of abandonment of this ground in the context of the abandonment of the six levels of gross and middling innate afflictions – these being abandoned on the path of meditation by means of the second through seventh grounds.[104]

In commenting, Chandrakirti does not clearly state either that the artificial afflictions are abandoned on the first ground or that the innate afflictions are abandoned from the second ground. However, Nagarjuna's *Precious Garland* explains that until the eighth ground is attained, the seeds of all afflictions are not removed [stanzas 455–6], that the conception of true existence is assigned as an affliction [stanza 35], that until that conception is removed the view of the transitory is not removed [stanza 35], and that the three links [view of the transitory collection as real 'I' and 'mine', afflicted doubt, and viewing bad ethics and codes of discipline as superior] are abandoned on the first ground [stanza 441]. Therefore, it is extremely clear that afflictions in general are divided into two [artificial and innate] and that the view of the transitory in particular must be divided in the same way.

In this system which identifies the conception of true existence as an affliction, when an affliction is abandoned by a noncontaminated path, a seed of the conception of true existence is necessarily abandoned. This abandonment can in no way remove a portion of the predispositions for erroneous dualistic appearance which are other than the seeds of the conception of true existence and which are assigned as the obstructions to omniscience. Therefore, the obstructions to omniscience are not abandoned until all the afflictions are extinguished. The obstructions to omniscience are abandoned on the three pure grounds [eighth, ninth, and tenth].

One abiding on the third ground has mostly become an Indra, chief of the gods. He has become skilled in an ability always to overcome the lustful desires of worldly sentient beings. Becoming a leader, he is skilled in removing sentient beings from the mud of desire.

The word 'also' appears in Nak-tso's translation as, 'He always abandons also lustful desire,' and this is most suitable.

DISTINGUISHING ATTRIBUTE OF THE FIRST THREE PERFECTIONS

Chandrakirti now clearly presents (1) the differences between those who are bases of [practising] the first three perfections, (2) the nature of the collections, and (3) the fruit that is achieved. His root text says:

39 *The Sugata mainly praised these three practices*
   Of giving, ethics, and patience for householders.
   These are also the collection of merit, the cause
   Of a Buddha Body the nature of which is form.

Both householder and monk Bodhisattvas are indeed bases of [practising] giving and so forth, but in terms of difficulty and ease of achievement, the three practices of giving, ethics, and patience are easier for householder Bodhisattvas to achieve. Therefore, the Sugata praised these three for them. Of the two collections, that of merit consists of these three. It is the predominant cause of a Buddha Body whose nature is form.

Nagarjuna's *Precious Garland* (399) says:

At that time [when you are a king] you should internalize
Firmly the practices of giving, ethics, and patience
Which were especially taught for householders
And which have an essence of compassion.

Among the three practices which are easy for householder Bodhisattvas, giving covers the donation of articles and bestowal of non-fright [taking bugs out of water, etc.]. Ethics is that of householders, and patience is mainly a mind determined about the doctrine. Effort, concentration, and wisdom are easier for monk Bodhisattvas, but this does not mean that householders and monks do not have the other three perfections.

The collection of wisdom consists of concentration and wisdom, which mainly cause the Truth Body. Effort is a cause of both collections.

CONCLUSION BY WAY OF EXPRESSING THE
FEATURES OF THE THIRD GROUND

Chandrakirti's root text says:

40 *Abiding in the sun which is the Conqueror Child,*
    The Luminous first completely dispels his darkness,
    Then seeks to overcome the darkness of migrators.
    On this ground, though very sharp, he does not get angry.

As soon as it is generated, the Luminous Ground abiding in the sun – the Bodhisattva – completely dispels the darkness of ignorance, included in his own continuum, that obstructs the arising of this ultimate ground. Through showing this aspect to others he then seeks to overcome the darkness obstructing the third ground for other migrators.

Because a Bodhisattva on the third ground overcomes the darkness of faults that destroy virtues, he becomes very sharp like the sun, but he does not get angry with faulty beings. This is because he has become extremely well accustomed to patience, and his continuum has been oiled with compassion.

Such is the explanation of the third ultimate mind generation in the *Illumination of the Thought, An Extensive Explanation of Chandrakirti's 'Supplement to the Middle Way'*.

12 Perfections of Effort and Concentration

FOURTH GROUND, THE RADIANT

This section has three parts, surpassing effort on the fourth ground, description of the ground, and features of abandonment.

SURPASSING EFFORT ON THE FOURTH GROUND

Now Chandrakirti indicates that on the fourth ground effort surpasses the first three perfections and is lower than the remaining six. His root text says:

41   *All attainments follow after effort,*
     Cause of the two collections of merit
     And wisdom. The ground where effort
     Flames is the fourth, the Radiant.

One who does not delight in virtue does not engage in all the various forms of giving and so forth; therefore, no attainments arise. However, for one who delights in accumulating or having accumulated the auspicious qualities of giving and so forth explained before, the qualities of attainments increase and qualities not yet attained are realized. All auspicious attainments follow after effort, the cause of the two collections of merit and wisdom. The ground where effort is said to flame increasingly is the fourth, called the Radiant.

On the third ground a training in higher meditative stabilization is attained that greatly exceeds that of the first two grounds. On the fourth ground a Bodhisattva thereby attains pliancy generated from meditative stabilization. This is a special factor totally removing laziness; hence, the perfection of effort is surpassing.

QUESTION: Why is this ground called the Radiant?
ANSWER: Chandrakirti's root text says:

42abc *There for the Sugata Child an illumination arises*
Produced from a greater cultivation of the harmonies
Of perfect enlightenment, surpassing the copper light.

On the fourth ground, an illumination of wisdom arises for a Sugata Child, produced from a more intense cultivation of the thirty-seven practices harmonious with perfect enlightenment. It surpasses the copper-like light described on the third ground. Since the intense light of the fire of true wisdom arises, this Bodhisattva ground is called the Radiant.

Chandrakirti's description in his *Supplement* is similar to Nagarjuna's explanation in his *Precious Garland* (447–8):

The fourth is called the Radiant
Because the light of true wisdom arises
In which he cultivates supremely
The harmonies of enlightenment.

Through the maturation of these qualities he becomes
A king of the gods in [the Land] Without Combat,
He is skilled in quelling the arising of the view
That the transitory collection [is a real self].

The thirty-seven harmonies with enlightenment are divided into seven groups:

I Four mindful establishments
  1 Mindful establishment on the body
  2 Mindful establishment on feeling

3 Mindful establishment on mind
4 Mindful establishment on phenomena

II Four thorough abandonings
  5 Generating virtuous qualities not yet generated
  6 Increasing virtuous qualities already generated
  7 Not generating non-virtuous qualities not yet generated
  8 Thoroughly abandoning non-virtuous qualities already
    generated

III Four legs of manifestation
  9 Aspiration
 10 Effort
 11 Thought
 12 Analytical meditative stabilization

IV Five faculties
 13 Faith
 14 Effort
 15 Mindfulness
 16 Meditative stabilization
 17 Wisdom

V Five powers
 18 Faith
 19 Effort
 20 Mindfulness
 21 Meditative stabilization
 22 Wisdom

VI Seven branches of enlightenment
 23 Correct mindfulness
 24 Correct discrimination of phenomena
 25 Correct effort
 26 Correct joy
 27 Correct pliancy
 28 Correct meditative stabilization
 29 Correct equanimity

VII Eightfold path
 30 Correct view
 31 Correct realization
 32 Correct speech

H

33 Correct aims of actions
34 Correct livelihood
35 Correct exertion
36 Correct mindfulness
37 Correct meditative stabilization.

The first group is the basis of training. In terms of the entities of the trainings, the second is in higher ethics, the third is in higher meditative stabilization, and the fourth through the sixth are in higher wisdom. On the fourth ground a Bodhisattva has the training in wisdom and becomes very skilled in the coarse and subtle thirty-seven harmonies with enlightenment.

FEATURES OF ABANDONMENT

Chandrakirti's root text says:

42d   *What is related to the view of a self is extinguished.*

The view of a self is the subtle view of the transitory collection, which precedes the coarse conceptions of a self of persons and of a person's belongings, and Chandrakirti refers to these latter as being related with a view of self. They are the conceptions that sentient beings and so forth exist substantially, self-sufficiently. Both this conception of a self of persons and that of phenomena – an adherence to the truth of the aggregates, constituents, and sources – are thoroughly extinguished.

   The meaning of 'extinguishment' is an abandonment of the seeds of the two conceptions of self that are to be abandoned on this ground and not extinguishment of all [forms of the two conceptions. For] the *Sutra on the Ten Grounds* indicates that [a fourth grounder] has the innate view of the transitory collection as a real 'I' and 'mine'.

Such is the explanation of the fourth ultimate mind generation in the *Illumination of the Thought, An Extensive Explanation of Chandrakirti's 'Supplement to the Middle Way'*.

FIFTH GROUND,
THE DIFFICULT TO OVERCOME

This section has two parts, (1) a description of the fifth ground and (2) surpassing concentration and skill in the truths.

DESCRIPTION OF THE FIFTH GROUND

Chandrakirti's root text says:

43ab *This great being on the ground Difficult to Overcome*
      Cannot be defeated even by all the demons.

This great being abiding on the fifth ground, the Difficult to Overcome, cannot be defeated even by all the *devaputra* demons[105] abiding in all the realms of the world. If so, what need is there to mention that he cannot be overcome by other demons such as Obeyers of [Demonic] Requests and Servant Demons? Therefore, the name of this ground is 'Difficult to Overcome'.

Nagarjuna's *Precious Garland* (449–50) says:

The fifth is called the Extremely Difficult to Overcome
Since all demons find it extremely hard to conquer him;
He becomes skilled in knowing the subtle
Meanings of the noble truths and so forth.

Through the maturation of these qualities he becomes
A king of the gods abiding in the Joyous Land,
He overcomes the sources of afflictions
And of the views of all the Forders.

SURPASSING CONCENTRATION AND
SKILL IN THE TRUTHS

Chandrakirti's root text says:

43cd *His concentration excels, and he attains great skill in knowledge*
      Of the subtle nature of the truths of those with a good mind.

On the fifth ground, from among the ten perfections, that of concentration is greatly surpassing. When Chandrakirti presents it thus [in his commentary][106], one should understand that since a Bodhisattva is known to have already attained the surpassing perfections of giving, ethics, patience, and effort, he is indicating that 'from among the latter six perfections the perfection of concentration is surpassing'. Here on the fifth ground a Bodhisattva has a measure of attainment with respect to complete non-oppression by faults discordant with the perfection of concentration, such as distraction and so on, that he does not have with respect to the perfections of wisdom and so forth.

Not only is his concentration surpassing, but also he attains great skill with respect to the subtle nature of the truths of those with a good mind – the truths of Superiors [the four noble truths] – which must be understood with a fine mind. Hence, he here comes to possess a higher wisdom which is comprised of skill in the coarse and subtle truths.

QUESTION: The *Sutra on the Ten Grounds* specifically sets forth that a fifth grounder is skilled in the four truths – sufferings, sources, cessations and paths – and in conventional truths and ultimate truths as well. However, the *Meeting of Father and Son Sutra (Pitāputrasamāgama)* and Nagarjuna's *Treatise on the Middle Way* (XXIV.8) say that truths are limited to two, conventional and ultimate. How could the four truths be separate from the two?

ANSWER: Chandrakirti explains in his commentary[107] that although there are no truths that are not included in the two, there is a purpose in setting out the four truths. It is done to indicate that the division of thoroughly afflicted phenomena which are to be abandoned consists of causes or sources, and effects or sufferings. Also, the division of very pure phenomena which are to be assumed consists of causes or true paths, and effects or true cessations. Furthermore, he explains that true sufferings, sources, and paths are conventional truths and that true cessations are ultimate truths.

Chandrakirti also explains in his commentary on Nagarjuna's *Sixty Stanzas of Reasoning* that nirvanas are ultimate truths and that the other three truths are conventional ones. Nirvanas are true cessations, and he adds that the Teacher,

Buddha, asserted that there is direct knowledge of true cessations. This is not feasible in the systems of proponents of true existence who assert that a direct valid cognizer has as its object an exclusively characterized [impermanent] phenomenon. In Chandrakirti's own system direct knowledge of cessation is established within the context of cognizing the meaning of suchness by way of a wisdom consciousness of uncontaminated meditative equipoise. Therefore, if true cessations were conventional truths, his presentation would be impossible. He also proves with great effort that when a nirvana is actualized, one must cognize the meaning of suchness directly. Therefore, those who propound that [according to Chandrakirti] true cessations are conventional truths have not come to the right decision.

Although an elimination of true existence – the object of negation – with respect to any base is considered an ultimate truth, it does not necessarily follow that the objects of negation of all ultimate truths do not exist among knowable objects. Nagarjuna's *Praise of the Element of Qualities* says:

Homage and obeisance to the element of qualities.
When it is not thoroughly understood,
One wanders in the three existences
Although it does in fact abide in all sentient beings.

Just this is also the Body of Truth
And the nirvana that is the purity
From having purified that which serves
As the cause of cyclic existence.

The nature of phenomena is accompanied with defilement, and when that is purified, Nagarjuna says that this nature becomes a nirvana and a Truth Body. There are many similar teachings that defilement is the object to be negated with respect to the purified nature of phenomena. If their nature could not become free from defilement, toil would be fruitless. Also, if the nature of phenomena can be freed from defilement, then its objects of negation can exist among knowable objects.

For example, in the non-existence of the horns of a rabbit these horns are the object of negation and do not occur among knowable objects. However, the non-existence of a pot – the negative of pot with pot as the object of negation and existing among knowable objects – can be posited as the non-existence of the horns of a rabbit.

In general, pure and impure phenomena are qualified by this nature [which is the absence of inherent existence], and in this context the negatives of the two selves, for instance, are negations in the sense that the object negated [inherent existence] simply does not occur among knowable objects. However, when the phenomena qualified by this nature are gradually purified of defilement, their nature also becomes purified. Therefore, with respect to a certain phenomenon qualified by this nature, it is not sufficient for its nature to be a partial purity, it must also be purified of the adventitious defilements which accord with a particular position [on the path]. These are called true cessations.

Many designations of truths such as skill in the truth of definitions and so forth occur with respect to this ground in the *Sutra on the Ten Grounds*. However, this does not mean that these are not included in the two truths.

Such is the explanation of the fifth mind generation in the *Illumination of the Thought, An Extensive Explanation of Chandrakirti's 'Supplement to the Middle Way'*.

Glossary

ENGLISH	SANSKRIT	TIBETAN
absorption	samāpatti	snyoms 'jug
action	karma	las
affliction	klesha	nyon mongs
altruism	parahita	gzhan la phan pa
analytical meditation		dpyad sgom
animal	tiryañch	dud 'gro
artificial	parikalpita	kun btags
aspect	ākāra	rnam pa
aspirational mind of enlightenment	bodhipraṇidhichitta	smon sems
bliss	sukha	bde ba
Blissful Pure Land	sukhāvatī	bde ba can
Bodhisattva	bodhisattva	byang chub sems dpa'
calm abiding	shamatha	zhi gnas
cause	hetu	rgyu
Chittamatra	chittamātra	sems tsam
clairvoyance	abhijñā	mngon par shes pa
common being	pṛthagjana	so so skye bo
compassion	karuṇā	snying rje
observing phenomena	dharmālambanā	chos la dmigs pa
observing sentient beings	sattvālambanā	sems can la dmigs pa
observing the unapprehendable	anālambanālambanā	dmigs med la dmigs pa
concentration	dhyāna	bsam gtan
conception of self	ātmagrāha	bdag tu 'dzin pa

ENGLISH	SANSKRIT	TIBETAN
condition	pratyaya	rkyen
Conqueror	jina	rgyal ba
consciousness	jña/ vijñāna	shes pa/ rnam par shes pa
constituent	dhātu	khams
contaminated action	sāsravakarma	zag bcas kyi las
contamination	āsrava	zag pa
continuum	saṃtāna	rgyud rgyun
conventional existence	saṃvṛtisat	kun rdzob tu yod pa
conventional mind generation	saṃvṛtichittotpāda	kun rdzob sems bskyed
conventional mind of enlightenment	saṃvṛtibodhichitta	kun rdzob byang chub kyi sems
conventional truth	saṃvṛtisatya	kun rdzob bden pa
co-operative cause	sahakāripratyaya	lhan cig byed rkyen
correct view	samyakdṛṣhṭi	yang dag pa'i lta ba
cyclic existence	saṃsāra	'khor ba
definite goodness	niḥshreyasa	nges legs
demigod	asura	lha ma yin
designation	vyavahāra	tha snyad
desire	rāga	'dod chags
desire realm	kāmadhātu	'dod khams
direct perception	pratyakṣha	mngon sum
discipline	vinaya	'dul ba
effort	vīrya	brtson 'grus
element of qualities	dharmadhātu	chos dbyings
Emanation Body	nirmāṇakāya	sprul pa'i sku
emptiness	shūnyatā	stong pa nyid
enlightenment	bodhi	byang chub
equanimity	upekṣhā	btang snyoms
ethics	shīla	tshul khrims
existence	sat	yod pa
extinguishment	kṣhaya	zad pa
five aggregates	pañchaskandha	phung po lnga
compositional factor	saṃskāra	'du byed
consciousness	vijñāna	rnam shes
discrimination	saṃjñā	'du shes
feeling	vedanā	tshor ba
form	rūpa	gzugs
Foe Destroyer	arhan	sgra bcom pa

ENGLISH	SANSKRIT	TIBETAN
Forder	tīrthika	mu stegs pa
Form Body	rūpakāya	gzugs sku
form realm	rūpadhātu	gzugs khams
formless realm	ārūpyadhātu	gzugs med khams
fruit	phala	'bras bu
generic image	arthasāmānya	don spyi
giving	dāna	sbyin pa
god	deva	lha
great compassion	mahākaruṇā	snying rje chen po
ground	bhūmi	sa
hatred	dveṣha	zhe sdang
Hearer	shrāvaka	nyan thos
hell-being	nāraka	dmyal ba pa
high status	abhyudaya	mngon mtho
human	manuṣhya	mi
hungry ghost	preta	yi dvags
ignorance	avidyā	ma rig pa
imputed existence	prajñaptisat	btags yod
individual emancipation	pratimokṣha	so so thar pa
inference	anumāṇa	rjes dpag
inherent existence	svabhāvasiddhi	rang bzhin gyis grub pa
innate	sahaja	lhan skyes
intelligence	buddhi/ mati	blo gros
Joyous Land	tuṣhita	dga' ldan
knowledge	abhidharma	chos mngon pa
Land of Controlling Others' Emanations	paranirmitashavartin	gzhan 'phrul dbang byed
Land of Liking Emanation	nirmāṇarati	'phrul dga'
Land of the Thirty-Three	trāyastriṃsha	sum bcu rtsa gsum
Land Without Combat	yāma	'thab bral
liberation	mokṣha	thar pa
lineage	gotra	rigs
love	maitri	byams pa

ENGLISH	SANSKRIT	TIBETAN
Madhyamika	Mādhyamika	dbu ma pa
meditative equipoise	samāhita	mnyam bzhag
meditative stabilization	samādhi	ting nge 'dzin
mental and physical aggregates	skandha	phung po
mental consciousness	manovijñāna	yid kyi rnam shes
mercy		rtse ba
merit	puṇya	bsod nams
method	upāya	thabs
migrator	gati	'gro ba
mind basis of all	ālayavijñāna	kun gzhi rnam shes
mind of enlightenment	bodhichitta	byang chub kyi sems
Mind-Only	chittamātra	sems tsam
momentariness	kṣhaṇika	skad cig ma
Most Tortuous Hell	avīchi	mnar med
natural existence	svalakṣhaṇasiddhi	rang gi mtshan nyid kyis grub pa
negation	pratiṣhedha	dgag pa
non-conceptual wisdom	nirvikalpajñāna	rnam par mi rtog pa'i ye shes
non-dual understanding		gnyis med kyi blo
non-product	asaṃskṛta	'dus ma byas
Nothingness	ākiṃchanya	ci yang med
object of negation	pratiṣhedhya	dgag bya
object of observation	ālambana	dmigs yul
obstructions to liberation/ afflictive obstructions	kleshāvaraṇa	nyon mongs pa'i sgrib pa
obstructions to omniscience	jñeyāvaraṇa	shes bya'i sgrib pa
omniscience	sarvākārajñāna	rnam pa thams cad mkhyen pa
path	mārga	lam
path of accumulation	saṃbhāramārga	tshogs lam
path of meditation	bhāvanāmārga	sgom lam
path of no more learning	ashaikṣhamārga	mi slob lam
path of preparation	prayogamārga	sbyor lam
path of seeing	darshanamārga	mthong lam
patience	kṣhānti	bzod pa
peak of cyclic existence	bhāvāgra	srid rtse

ENGLISH	SANSKRIT	TIBETAN
perfection	pāramitā	pha rol tu phyin pa
person	pudgala	gang zag
phenomenon	dharma	chos
potency	vāsanā	bag chags
practical mind of		'jug sems
enlightenment		
Prasangika- Madhyamika	prāsaṅgika-mādhyamika	dbu ma thal 'gyur pa
predisposition/ latent	vāsanā	bag chags
predisposition		
product	saṃskṛta	'dus byas
referent object		zhen yul
Reviving Hell	saṃjīva	yang sos
self-sufficient		rang rkya ba
selflessness	nairātmya	bdag med
selflessness of persons	pudgalanairātmya	gang zag gi bdag med
selflessness of phenomena	dharmanairātmya	chos kyi bdag med
sentient being	sattva	sems can
sets of discourses	sūtrānta	mdo sde
Solitary Realizer	pratyekabuddha/ svajina	rang sangs rgyas/ rang rgyal
special insight	vipashyanā	lhag mthong
stabilizing meditation		'jog sgom
Stream Enterer	shrotāpanna	rgyun zhugs
substantial cause	upādāna	nyer len
substantial existence	dravyasat	rdzas yod
suchness	tathatā	de kho na nyid
suffering of change	vipariṇāmaduḥkhatā	'gyur ba'i sdug bsngal
suffering of composition	saṃskāraduḥkhatā	'du byed kyi sdug bsngal
suffering of pain	duḥkhaduḥkhatā	sdug bsngal gyi sdug bsngal
Superior	āryan	'phags pa
supramundane	lokottara	'jig rten las 'das pa
Svatantrika- Madhyamika	svātantrika- mādhyamika	dbu ma rang rgyud pa
ten grounds	dashabhūmi	sa bcu
1 very joyful	pramuditā	rab tu dga' ba
2 stainless	vimalā	dri ma med pa
3 luminous	prabhākarī	'od byed pa
4 radiant	archiṣhmatī	'od 'phro ba

ENGLISH	SANSKRIT	TIBETAN
5 difficult to overcome	sudurjayā	sbyang dka' ba
6 manifest	abhimukhī	mngon du gyur pa
7 gone afar	dūraṃgama	ring du song ba
8 immovable	achalā	mi g.yo ba
9 good intelligence	sādhumatī	legs pa'i blo gros
10 cloud of doctrine	dharmameghā	chos kyi sprin
tenet/system of tenets	siddhānta	grub mtha'
Three Refuges	trisharaṇa	skyabs gsum
Truth Body	dharmakāya	chos sku
ultimate mind generation	paramārthabodhi- chittotpāda	don dam byang chub kyi sems bskyed
ultimate mind of enlightment	paramārthabodhi- chitta	don dam byang chub kyi sems
ultimate truth	paramārthasatya	don dam bden pa
unusual attitude	adhyāshaya	lhag bsam
Vaibhashika	vaibhāṣhika	bye brag smra ba
valid cognition	pramāṇa	tshad ma
vehicle	yāna	theg pa
view	dṛṣhṭi	lta ba
view of the transitory collection	satkāyadṛṣhṭi	'jig tshogs la lta ba
wind	prāṇa/ vāyu	rlung
wisdom	prajñā	shes rab
wrong view	mithyādṛṣhṭi	log lta
Yogachara-Svatantrika- Madhyamika	yogāchāra- svātantrika- mādhyamika	rnal 'byor spyod pa'i dbu ma rang rgyud pa

Bibliography

Here and in the notes, with regard to works found in the Tibetan canon, "P" refers to the *Tibetan Tripitaka* (Tokyo-Kyoto: Suzuki Research Foundation, 1956), which is a reprint of the Peking edition. The English titles are usually abbreviated.

1 SUTRAS

Akashagarbha Sutra
　Ākāshagarbha
　Nam mkha'i snying po
　P926, vol. 36

Array of Stalks Sutra
　Gaṇḍavyūha
　sDong po bkod pa
　[?]

Aspirational Prayers for Auspicious Deeds
　Bhadrachāryapraṇidhānarāja
　bZang po spyod pa'i smon lam gyi rgyal po
　P716, vol. 11

Brief Scriptures on Discipline
　Vinayakṣhudravastu
　'Dul ba phran tshegs kyi gzhi
　P1035, vol. 44

Cloud of Jewels Sutra
　Ratnamegha

dKon mchog sprin
P897, vol. 35

Compendium of All the Weaving Sutra
Sarvavaidalyasaṃgraha
rNam par 'thag pa thams cad bsdus pa
P893, vol. 35

Condensed Perfection of Wisdom Sutra
Sañchayagāthāprajñāpāramitā
Shes rab kyi pha rol tu phyin pa sdud pa tshigs su bcad pa
P735, vol. 21

Diamond Cutter Sutra
Vajrachchhedikā
rDo rje gcod pa
P739, vol. 21

Great Drum Sutra
Mahābherīhārakaparivarta
rNga bo che chen po'i le'u
P888, vol. 35

King of Meditations Sutra
Samādhirāja/ Sarvadharmasvabhāvasamatāvipañchitasamādhirāja
Ting nge 'dzin rgyal po/ Chos thams cad kyi rang bzhin mnyam
pa nyid rnam par spros pa ting nge 'dzin gyi rgyal po
P795, vol. 31–2

Liberation of Maitreya Sutra
Maitreyavimokṣha
Byams pa'i rnam thar
[?]

Lion's Roar of Maitreya Sutra
Maitreyamahāsiṃhanāda
Byams pa'i seng ge'i sgra chen po
P760 (23), vol. 24

Manjushri Sport Sutra
Mañjushrīvikrīḍita
'Jam dpal rnam par rol pa
P764, vol. 27

Meeting of Father and Son Sutra
Pitāputrasamāgama
Yab dang sras mjal ba
P760 (16), vol. 23

Moon Lamp Sutra; see *King of Meditations Sutra*

Omnipresent Doctrine Sutra
[?]
Chos kun 'gro ba
[?]

One Hundred Thousand Stanza Perfection of Wisdom Sutra
Shatasāhasrikāprajñāpāramitā
Shes rab kyi pha rol tu phyin pa stong phrag brgya pa
P730, vol. 12

Pile of Jewels Sutra
Mahāratnakūṭadharmaparyāyashatasāhasrikagrantha
dKon mchog brtsegs pa chen po'i chos kyi rnam grangs le'u stong phrag brgya pa
P760, vol. 22

Questions of Adhyashaya Sutra
Adhyāshayasaṃchodana
Lhag pa'i bsam pa bskul ba
P760 (25), vol. 24

Questions of Gaganaganja Sutra
Gaganagañjaparipṛchchhā
Nam mkha'i mdzod kyis zhus pa
P815, vol. 33

Questions of Upali Sutra
Upāliparipṛchchhā
Nye bar 'khor gyis zhus pa
[?]

Sutra on Manjushri's Buddha Land
Mañjushrībuddhakṣhetraguṇavyūha
'Jam dpal gyi sangs rgyas kyi zhing gi yon tan bkod pa
P760 (15), vol. 23

Sutra on the Generation of the Power of Faith
Shraddhābalādhānāvatāramudrā

Dad pa'i stobs bskyed pa la 'jug pa'i phyag rgya
P867, vol. 34

Sutra on the Miserliness of One in Trance
Dhyāyitamuṣṭi
bSam gtan dpe mkhyud
[?]

Sutra on the Ten Grounds
Dashabhūmika
mDo sde sa bcu pa
P761 (31), vol. 25

Teaching of Akshayamati Sutra
Akṣhayamatinirdesha
bLo gros mi zad pas bstan pa
P842, vol. 34

Topics of Discipline
Vinayavastu
'Dul ba gzhi
P1030, vol. 41

Two Thousand Five Hundred Stanza Perfection of Wisdom Sutra
Sārdhadvisāhasrikāprajñāpāramitā/ Suvikrāntavikramiparipṛch-
chhā
Shes rab kyi pha rol tu phyin pa gnyis stong lnga rgya pa/ Rab
kyi tshal gyis rnam par gnon pas zhus pa
P736, vol. 21

White Lotus of Excellent Doctrine Sutra
Saddharmapuṇḍarīka
Dam pa'i chos pad ma dkar po
P781, vol. 30

2 OTHER WORKS

Ajitamitra (Mi-pham-bshes-gnyen). *Commentary on the Precious
Garland*
Ratnāvalīṭīkā
Rin po che'i phreng ba'i rgya cher bshad pa
P5659, vol. 129

Āryadeva ('Phags-pa-lha). *Four Hundred*
Chatuḥshatakashāstrakārikā
bsTan bcos bzhi brgya pa zhes bya ba'i tshig le'ur byas pa
P5246, vol. 95

Āryavimuktisena ('Phags-pa-grol-sde). *Illumination of the Twenty-Five Thousand Stanza Perfection of Wisdom*
Pañchaviṃshatisāhasrikāprajñāpāramitopadeshashāstrābhisamayā-laṃkāravṛtti
Shes rab kyi pha rol tu phyin pa stong phrag nyi shu lnga pa'i man ngag gi bstan bcos mngon par rtogs pa'i rgyan gyi 'grel pa
P5185, vol. 88

Asaṅga (Thogs-med). *Bodhisattva Levels*
Yogacharyābhūmau bodhisattvabhūmi
rNal 'byor spyod pa'i sa las byang chub sems dpa'i sa
P5538, vol. 110

Asaṅga *Compendium of Knowledge*
Abhidharmasamuchchaya
mNgon pa kun btus
P5550, vol. 112

Atīsha. *Lamp for the Path to Enlightenment*
Bodhipathapradīpa
Byang chub lam gyi sgron ma
P5343, vol. 103

Bhāvaviveka (Legs-ldan-'byed). *Blaze of Reasoning*
Madhyamakahṛdayavṛttitarkajvālā
dbU ma'i snying po'i 'grel pa rtog ge 'bar ba
P5256, vol. 96

Bhāvaviveka. *Essence of the Middle Way*
Madhyamakahṛdayakārikā
dbU ma'i snying po'i tshig le'ur byas pa
P5255, vol. 96

Bhāvaviveka. *Lamp for Wisdom*
Prajñāpradīpamūlamadhyamakavṛtti
dbU ma rtsa ba'i 'grel pa shes rab sgron ma
P5253, vol. 95

Buddhapālita (Sangs-rgyas-bskyangs). *Buddhapalita's Commentary on the Treatise on the Middle Way*
Buddhapālitamūlamadhyamakavṛtti
dbU ma rtsa ba'i 'grel pa buddha pā li ta
P5242, vol. 95

Chandrakīrti (Zla-ba-grags-pa). *Clear Words*
Mūlamadhyamakavṛttiprasannapadā
dbU ma rtsa ba'i 'grel pa tshig gsal ba
P5260, vol. 98

Chandrakīrti. *Commentary on the Four Hundred*
Bodhisattvayogacharyāchatuḥshatakaṭīkā
Byang chub sems dpa'i rnal 'byor spyod pa bzhi brgya pa'i rgya cher 'grel pa
P5266, vol. 98

Chandrakīrti. *Commentary on the Sixty Stanzas of Reasoning*
Yuktishaṣhṭikāvṛtti
Rigs pa drug cu pa'i 'grel pa
P5265, vol. 98

Chandrakīrti. *Commentary on the Supplement to the Middle Way*
Madhyamakāvatārabhāṣhya
dbU ma la 'jug pa'i bshad pa
P5263, vol. 98
Also: (Dharmsala: The Council of Cultural & Religious Affairs of His Holiness the Dalai Lama, 1968)

Chandrakīrti. *Seventy Stanzas on the Three Refuges*
Trisharaṇasaptati
gSum la skyabs su 'gro ba bdun cu pa
P5366, vol. 103

Chandrakīrti. *Supplement to the Middle Way*
Madhyamakāvatāra
dbU ma la 'jug pa
P5261, 5262, vol. 98

Dharmakīrti (Chos-kyi-grags-pa). *Commentary on the Compendium on Valid Cognition*
Pramāṇavarttikakārikā
Tshad ma rnam 'grel gyi tshig le'ur byas pa
P5709, vol. 130

Fifth Dalai Lama (Ngag-dbang-blo-bzang-rgya-mtsho). *Sacred Word of Manjushri*
Byang chub lam gyi rim pa'i 'khrid yig 'jam pa'i dbyangs kyi zhal lung
(Thim phu: Kun bzang stobs rgyal, 1976)

Gyel-tsap (rGyal-tshab). *Explanation of Engaging in the Bodhisattva Deeds, Entrance of Buddha Conqueror Children*
Byang chub sems dpa'i spyod pa la 'jug pa'i rnam bshad rgyal sras 'jug ngog
(Sarnath: Pleasure of Elegant Sayings Printing Press, 1973)

Haribhadra (Seng-ge-bzang-po). *Clear Meaning Commentary*
Abhisamayālaṃkāranāmaprajñāpāramitopadeshashāstravṛtti
Shes rab kyi pha rol tu phyin pa'i man ngag gi bstan bcos mngon par rtogs pa'i rgyan ces bya ba'i 'grel pa
P5191, vol. 90

Haribhadra. *Great Commentary on the Eight Thousand Stanza Perfection of Wisdom Sutra*
Aṣṭasāhasrikāprajñāpāramitāvyākyānābhisamayālaṃkārāloka
Shes rab kyi pha rol tu phyin pa brgyad stong pa'i bshad pa mngon par rtogs pa'i rgyan gyi snang ba
P5189, vol. 90

Hopkins, Paul Jeffrey. *Meditation on Emptiness* (Ann Arbor: University Microfilms, 1973)

Jam-yang-shay-ba ('Jam-dbyangs-bzhad-pa). *Great Exposition of the Middle Way*
dbU ma la 'jug pa'i mtha' dpyod lung rigs gter mdzod zab don kun gsal skal bzang 'jug ngog
(Buxaduor: Gomang, 1967)

Jaya-ānanda. *Explanation of the Supplement to the Middle Way*
Madhyamakāvatāraṭīkā
dbU ma la 'jug pa'i 'grel bshad
P5271, vol. 99

Kamalashīla. *Stages of Meditation*
Bhāvanākrama
sGom pa'i rim pa
P5310–12, vol. 102

Kön-chok-jik-may-wang-po (dKon-mchog-'jigs-med-dbang-po).
Presentation of the Grounds and Paths
   Sa dang lam gyi rnam par bzhag pa
   Collected Works (New Delhi: Ngawang Gelek Demo, 1971)

La Vallee Poussin, Louis de. 'Madhyamakāvatāra', *Museon*, NS
1907

Maitreya (Byams-pa). *Discrimination of Phenomena and the Nature of
Phenomena*
   Dharmadharmatāvibhaṅga
   Chos dang chos nyid rnam par 'byed pa
   P5523, vol. 108

Maitreya. *Discrimination of the Middle Way and the Extremes*
   Madhyāntavibhaṅga
   dbUs dang mtha' rnam par 'byed pa
   P5522, vol. 108

Maitreya. *Ornament for the Mahayana Sutras*
   Mahāyānasūtrālaṃkārakārikā
   Theg pa chen po'i mdo sde rgyan gyi tshig le'ur byas pa
   P5521, vol. 108

Maitreya. *Ornament for the Realizations*
   Abhisamayālaṃkāra
   mNgon par rtogs pa'i rgyan
   P5184, vol. 88

Maitreya. *Sublime Science*
   Mahāyānottaratantrashāstra
   Theg pa chen po rgyud bla ma'i bstan bcos
   P5525, vol. 108

Nāgārjuna. (kLu-sgrub). *Compendium of Sutra*
   Sūtrasamuchchaya
   mDo kun las btus pa
   P5330, vol. 102

Nāgārjuna. *Essay on the Mind of Enlightenment*
   Bodhichittavivaraṇa
   Byang chub sems kyi 'grel pa
   P2665, 2666, vol. 61

Nāgārjuna. *Friendly Letter*
Suhṛllekha
bShes pa'i spring yig
P5682, vol. 129

Nāgārjuna. *Praise of the Element of Qualities*
Dharmadhātustotra
Chos kyi dbyings su bstod pa
P2010, vol. 46

Nāgārjuna. *Praise of the Supramundane*
Lokātītastava
'Jig rten las 'das par bstod pa
P2012, vol. 46

Nāgārjuna. *Six Collections of Reasoning*
 Precious Garland of Advice for the King
  Rājaparikathāratnāvalī
  rGyal po la gtam bya ba rin po che'i phreng ba
  P5658, vol. 129
  Also: (London: Allen and Unwin, 1975)
 Refutation of Objections
  Vigrahavyāvartanīkārikā
  rTsod pa bzlong pa'i tshig le'ur byas pa
  P5228, vol. 95
 Seventy Stanzas on Emptiness
  Shūnyatāsaptatikārikā
  sTong pa nyid bdun cu pa'i tshig le'ur byas pa
  P5227, vol. 95
 Sixty Stanzas of Reasoning
  Yuktiṣhaṣhṭikākārikā
  Rigs pa drug cu pa'i tshig le'ur byas pa
  P5225, vol. 95
 Treatise Called 'The Finely Woven'
  Vaidalyasūtranāma
  Zhib mo rnam par 'thag pa zhes bya ba'i mdo
  P5226, vol. 95
 Treatise on the Middle Way
  Prajñānāmamūlamadhyamakakārikā/ Madhyamakashāstra
  dbU ma rtsa ba'i tshig le'ur byas pa shes rab ces bya ba/ dbU

ma'i bstan bcos
P5224, vol. 95

Na-wang-bel-den (Ngag-dbang-dpal-ldan). *Explanation of the Conventional and the Ultimate in the Four Systems of Tenets*
Grub mtha' bzhi'i lugs kyi kun rdzob dang don dam pa'i don rnam par bshad pa legs bshad dpyid kyi dpal mo'i glu dbyangs
(New Delhi: Guru Deva, 1972)

Pan-chen-sö-nam-trak-pa (Paṇ-chen-bsod-nams-grags-pa). *Root Text Commentary on the Ornament for the Realizations*
Phar phyin rtsa ṭīk
(Buxa: Nang bstan shes rig 'dzin skyong slob gnyer khang, 1964)

Pāṇini. *The Aṣṭadhyāyi of Pāṇini*, ed. and trans. S. C. Vasu (Delhi: Motilal, 1962)

Prajñākaramati (Shes-rab-'byung-gnas-blo-gros). *Commentary on the Difficult Points of Engaging in the Bodhisattva Deeds*
Bodhicharyāvatārapañjikā
Byang chub kyi spyod pa la 'jug pa'i dka' 'grel
P5273, vol. 100

Ratnadāsa (dKon-mchog-dbyangs). *Praise of Endless Qualities*
Guṇaparyantastotra
Yon tan mtha' yas par stod pa
P2044, vol. 46

Shāntideva (Zhi-ba-lha). *Compendium of Instructions*
Shikṣhāsamuchchayakārikā
bsLab pa kun las btus pa'i tshig le'ur byas pa
P5336, vol. 102. Also: ed. C. Bendall, Bibliotheca Buddhica (Osnabruck: Biblio Verlag, 1970)

Shāntideva. *Engaging in the Bodhisattva Deeds*
Bodhisattvacharyāvatāra
Byang chub sems dpa'i spyod pa la 'jug pa
P5272, vol. 99

Shāntirakṣhita (Zhi-ba-'tsho). *Ornament of the Middle Way*
Madhyamakālaṃkārakārikā
dbU ma'i rgyan gyi tshig le'ur byas pa
P5284, vol. 101

Sopa and Hopkins. *Practice and Theory of Tibetan Buddhism* (London: Rider, 1976)

Tsong-ka-pa (Tsong-kha-pa). *Great Exposition of the Stages of the Path*
skyes bu gsum gyi nyams su blang pa'i rim pa thams cad tshang bar ston pa'i byang chub lam gyi rim pa
P6001, vol. 152

Tsong-ka-pa. *Illumination of the Thought, An Extensive Explanation of Chandrakirti's 'Supplement to the Middle Way'*
dbU ma la 'jug pa'i rgya cher bshad pa dgongs pa rab gsal
P6143, vol. 154
The edition used for the translation in Part Two is: (Dharamsala: Tibetan Cultural Printing Press, no date)

Vasubandhu (dbYig-gnyen). *Treasury of Knowledge*
Abhidharmakoshakārikā
Chos mngon pa'i mdzod kyi tshig le'ur byas pa
P5590, vol. 115

Notes

Here and in the bibliography, with regard to works found in the Tibetan canon, 'P' refers to the *Tibetan Tripitaka* (Tokyo-Kyoto: Suzuki Research Foundation, 1956), which is a reprint of the Peking edition.

Abbreviations used:
Comm: *Commentary on the Supplement to the Middle Way* by Chandrakirti
GM: *Great Exposition of the Middle Way* by Jam-yang-shay-ba
Pāṇ: *The Aṣhṭadhyāyi of Pāṇini*
Complete entries for the above texts may be found in the bibliography.

1 According to Lati Rinbochay, those on the three levels are beings below, on, and above the earth, or those of the desire, form, and formless realms.
2 Those gone to bliss, that is, Buddhas.
3 Nagarjuna.
4 He took rebirth in a land favourable to the achievement of tantra.
5 According to Lati Rinbochay, these are the commentaries on Nagarjuna's *Treatise on the Middle Way* by Buddhapalita, Bhavaviveka, and Chandrakirti.
6 *Comm*, 2.3.
7 The reference is to Jaya-ananda's view as given in his commentary to the *Supplement*. See *GM*, 5a.3.
8 *GM*, 4a.1 ff.
9 *GM*, 6a.2.
10 *Comm*, 315.19.
11 *Comm*, 316.3.
12 Tsong-ka-pa's teacher Ren-da-wa (Red-mda'-ba) asserted that Nagarjuna's *Treatise* is common to both Hinayana and Mahayana because it does not set forth the Mahayana paths. See *GM*, 14b.2.
13 *Comm*, 20.13.
14 Manjushri has the form of a sixteen year old.
15 Kensur Lekden reported that during the rule (815–38) of the Tibetan king Tri-ral-wa-jen (Khri-ral-pa-can), it was decided to salute Manjushri at the beginning of presentations of wisdom – mainly found in the knowledge

(*abhidharma*) division – because Manjushri is the physical manifestation of the wisdom of all Buddhas. It was also decided to salute Buddha and the Bodhisattvas at the beginning of presentations of meditative stabilization – mainly found in the sets of discourses (*sūtrānta*) – because these were set forth by both Buddha and Bodhisattvas. The Omniscient One is saluted at the beginning of presentations of ethics – mainly found in the discipline (*vinaya*) – because these were set forth only by Buddha since he made the rulings. Despite this formulation, it was not always followed, many translators choosing to pay homage to their protective deity.

16 *GM*, 17b.4. For Jaya-ananda's interpretation see *GM*, 17a.6. See *Comm*, 3.14.
17 *Comm*, 4.2.
18 Jam-yang-shay-ba (*GM*, 18b.6) refers to Chandrakirti's *Seventy Stanzas on the Three Refuges* and his *Commentary on (Aryadeva's) Four Hundred* as well as the *Great Drum Sutra* (*Mahābherihāraka*).
19 *GM*, 19a.3. The parenthetical explanation is from *GM*, 19a.2.
20 *GM*, 19b.2.
21 *Comm*, 4.5.
22 *Comm*, 4.7.
23 *GM*, 25a.4.
24 *GM*, 19b.5.
25 *Comm*, 3.1–11: 'There are some [that is, Solitary Realizers] who, though they have become skilled in realizing the ultimate from only hearing the teaching of dependent-arising, do not attain nirvana in just this lifetime. Nevertheless, it is certain that practitioners of the teaching will attain a fruition of the wished for effect in another lifetime, as is the case with the effect [of an action] the fruition of which is definite. Aryadeva says:

> Though one who knows suchness does not achieve
> Nirvana here, in another birth
> He will definitely attain it
> Without effort, as in the case of actions.

Therefore, [Nagarjuna's *Treatise on the*] *Middle Way* (XVIII.12) also says:

> Though the perfect Buddhas do not appear
> And Hearers have disappeared,
> A Solitary Realizer's wisdom
> Arises without support.

Kensur Lekden reported that there are three types of Solitary Realizers:

1 rhinoceros-like Solitary Realizer, who accumulates the collections of merit in the presence of a Buddha for a hundred great aeons, but then in one lifetime actualizes the remaining four paths of preparation, seeing, meditation, and no more learning without depending on a teacher. During his last lifetime he attains the four fruits of Stream Enterer, Once Returner, Never Returner, and Foe Destroyer.
2 greater congregating Solitary Realizer, who attains the first three fruits – Stream Enterer, Once Returner, and Never Returner – in the presence

of a Buddha, and then in his last lifetime actualizes the fruit of Foe Destroyer alone without depending on a teacher.

3 lesser congregating Solitary Realizer, who attains the first three of the four levels on the path of preparation – heat, peak, and forbearance – but not the fourth, supreme qualities, in the presence of a Buddha and then actualizes the remaining paths (including the four fruits) alone.

Kensur Lekden reported that Hearers who have the simultaneous mode of abandonment, passing through the path of meditation in nine stages rather than eighty-one as in gradual abandonment, can become Solitary Realizers if it so happens that in their last lifetime they do not meet with a Buddha. This, then, would be the referent in the quote from Nagarjuna above.

26 *GM*, 20a.3.
27 Jam-yang-shay-ba traces this criticism of Chandrakirti to 'a Tibetan' (*GM*, 30b.4) but does not identify him.
28 *Comm*, 4.14–17.
29 *Comm*, 6.20. Poussin ('Madhyamakāvatāra,' *Museon*, NS 1907, vol. VIII, p. 263, n2) conjectures that the sutra may be the *Āryadharmasaṃgiti-sūtra*. For the quote, see *Comm*, 6.8–20. Tsong-ka-pa paraphrases the sutra.
30 *Comm*, 7.17.
31 *Comm*, 10.9–12.
32 'Mind generation is the wish for complete / Perfect enlightenment for the sake of others.' I.18.
33 Tsong-ka-pa paraphrases *Comm*, 6.2.
34 *Comm*, 5.9–17.
35 *Comm*, 6.7.
36 *GM*, 38b.5.
37 *Comm*, 7.20.
38 *Comm*, 8.16
39 The twelve links of dependent-arising in cyclic existence.
40 Actions impelling rebirth in the form and formless realms are called 'unmoving' because, unlike meritorious and non-meritorious actions, their fruition cannot move or shift to another type, as is the case when a non-meritorious action impelling an animal birth bears, instead, the fruit of stupidity within a human existence.
41 *Comm*, 9.15.
42 *Comm*, 10.3–5.
43 *Comm*, 9.13.
44 *GM*, 56b.4
45 The view of common personal selflessness is that of the non-substantial or self-sufficient existence of persons; it is called 'common' because of being shared with the other systems, not being peculiar to the Prasangika system. The view of suchness is of the emptiness of inherent existence and is found only in the Prasangika system.
46 *Comm*, 10.2.
47 The happiness of the happy migrations of humans and gods.
48 According to Kön-chok-jik-may-wang-po (*Presentation of the Grounds and*

Paths, Collected Works [New Delhi: Ngawang Gelek Demo, 1971], VII, 426.3), the eight levels of Hearers are:

1 level of seeing the wholesome, which is the Hearer path of accumulation, this being the initial attainment of pure phenomena
2 level of lineage, which is the Hearer path of preparation, when a non-mistakenness is attained with respect to one's lineage
3 level of the eighth which is the Hearer realization of approaching to Stream Enterer, the attainment of the first of the eight levels of approaching to and abiding in the fruits of Stream Enterer, Once Returner, Never Returner, and Foe Destroyer
4 level of seeing, which is the Hearer realization of abiding in the fruit of Stream Enterer; according to the Yogachara-Svatantrikas this is when one newly sees the selflessness of the person with a supramundane path consciousness, which according to the Prasangikas, however, occurs with the attainment of approaching to Stream Enterer
5 level of diminishment, which is the Hearer realization of abiding in the fruit of Once Returner, when the first six of the nine afflictions related with the desire realm have been abandoned
6 level of separation from desire, which is the Hearer realization of abiding in the fruit of Never Returner, when one has separated from all afflictions related with the desire realm
7 level of realizing completion, which is the Hearer realization of Foe Destroyer, when one has completed the activities of one's own path
8 level of Solitary Realizer, which refers to the realizations of Solitary Realizers, including all levels of their path.

49 *Comm*, 10.14.
50 *Comm*, 10.18.
51 *GM*, 72a.3.
52 P5260, vol. 98 7.5.7 ff.
53 *Comm*, 11.13.
54 *Comm*, 10.20.
55 Kön-chok-jik-may-wang-po, *Presentation of the Grounds and Paths*, Collected Works (New Delhi: Ngawang Gelek Demo, 1971), VII, 458 ff.
56 *GM*, 76b.4.
57 See note 55.
58 *Comm*, 11.20.
59 Quoting the *Sutra on the Generation of the Power of Faith (Shraddhābalā-dhānāvatāramudrā)*: see *GM*, 82a.2. Original text is P867, vol. 34 278.5.2.
60 Tsong-ka-pa is paraphrasing *Comm*, 12.5–13.
61 'Subtle increasers' (*anushaya, phra rgyas*) are the root afflictions – desire, anger, pride, ignorance, doubt, and afflicted view. According to Lati Rinbochay, these are 'subtle' in that they have beginninglessly been difficult to identify and are 'increasers' because either as objects of observation or as mental accompaniers they increase contaminations.
62 Abider in and approacher to the fruits of Foe Destroyer, Never Returner, Once Returner, and Stream Enterer.
63 Literally, 'garudas.'

64 *GM,* 83b.2.

65 *GM,* 84a.5 – 86a.4.

66 *Comm,* 17.10–13.

67 *GM,* 88b.5. This is discussed from 88b.2 – 89a.2.

68 *GM,* 118b.2.

69 The non-view afflictions include the remaining five root afflictions – desire, anger, pride, ignorance, and doubt – as well as the twenty secondary afflictions – belligerence, resentment, concealment, spite, jealousy, miserliness, deceit, dissimulation, haughtiness, harmfulness, non-shame, non-embarrassment, lethargy, excitement, non-faith, laziness, non-conscientiousness, forgetfulness, non-introspection, and distraction.

70 *Comm,* 17.15–20.

71 The translation of the stanzas depends heavily on Gyel-tsap's commentary, *Explanation of Engaging in the Bodhisattva Deeds, Entrance of Conqueror Children* (Sarnath: Pleasure of Elegant Sayings Printing Press, 1973), 230.14 – 237.1

72 *GM,* 120b.3 – 121.b.3.

73 As identified in Na-wang-bel-den, *Explanation of the Con ntional and the Ultimate in the Four Systems of Tenets* (New Delhi: Guru Deva, 1972), 616.7.

74 *GM,* 119b.1.

75 *GM,* 116b.5 – 117a.3.

76 Lati Rinbochay reported that some Tibetan scholars consider the text here to be corrupt and thus remove the negative (*ma*), as has been done in this translation.

77 *Comm,* 18.1.

78 Poussin (op.cit., p. 271, n.1) says 'Voir *Saṃyuttanikāya* III, p.142.'

79 *GM,* 188a.3.

80 Chandrakirti, *Clear Words,* P5263, vol. 98, 43.5.7.

81 *Comm,* 20.1–4.

82 The Peking edition (P6143, vol. 154, 17.2.7) has *zad pa* (extinguishment) for *thar pa* (liberation). Both appear in Tsong-ka-pa's commentary. Nagarjuna's text itself is P2012, vol. 46, 34.2.8.

83 According to Pan-chen-sö-nam-trak-pa (*Root Text Commentary on [Maitreya's] 'Ornament for the Realizations'* [Buxa: Nang bstan shes rig 'dzin skyong slob gnyer khang, 1964] 103a.3ff), true cessations in the continuums of Hearer Foe Destroyers are purities of 'student' Hearers due to being abandonments of afflictions. True cessations in the continuums of Solitary Realizer Foe Destroyers are purities of rhinoceros-like Solitary Realizers due to being abandonments of the coarse obstructions to objects of knowledge, that is, to omniscience. True cessations of second ground Bodhisattvas are purities of Conqueror Children due to being diminishments of obstructions to the three paths – Hearer, Solitary Realizer, and Mahayana.

84 Poussin (p. 276, n.3) says, 'Même texte, extrait du *Gaganagañjasūtra* dans *Cikṣhāsamuccaya,* p. 272.5–8.' Original text is P815, vol. 33, 6.5.1–3.

85 Shorea Robusta.

86 *Comm,* 26.9.

87 *Pāṇ*, VI.3.1: alug uttarapade.
88 *Pāṇ*, VI.3.109: prṣhodaradini yathopadiṣhtam.
89 The meaning of this sentence is obscure. Jam-yang-shay-ba does not comment on it.
90 Text reads *am*, which has been edited to accord with *GM*, 148a.3–5.
91 According to Kalāpa, the nominative singular is *si*, whereas for Chandragomin and others it is *su*; thus, Tsong-ka-pa appears to be following Kalāpa. See Paul Jeffrey Hopkins, *Meditation on Emptiness* (Ann Arbor: University Microfilms, 1973), p. 829.
92 *Comm*, 40.14.
93 *Comm*, 40.14.
94 *Comm*, 42.10 – 43.4.
95 *GM*, 159a.5.
96 According to Gyel-tsap's commentary (22.4) 'patron' here refers to one who gives all help and happiness.
97 Translation follows the Sanskrit: Shantideva, *Cikṣhāsamuccaya*, ed. C. Bendall, Bibliotheca Buddhica (Osnabruck: Biblio Verlag, 1970), I, 149.1.
98 *GM*, 164a.3.
99 *Comm*, 42.15.
100 The reference is to Bu-tön (Bu-ston) according to *GM*, 160a.5.
101 Kensur Lekden identified these as the powers of (1) contrition, (2) engaging in an antidote (any virtuous activity), (3) refraining from the non-virtue in the future, and (4) a base (such as Vajrasattva to whom non-virtue is revealed).
102 See stanza 411 in *The Precious Garland* (London: Allen and Unwin, 1975).
103 *Comm*, 50.7.
104 See Sopa and Hopkins, *Practice and Theory of Tibetan Buddhism* (London: Rider, 1976), p. 87.
105 These demons especially block elevation above the desire realm and progress to liberation.
106 *Comm*, 57.8.
107 *Comm*, 58.4.

Index